**When life is pulling you in all directions...
when problems overshadow your dreams...
turn to these books for guidance and
affirmation:**

Stressed-Out But Hangin' Tough by **Andrea Stephens**
An easy-to-read guide to help overcome the pressures that
can sometimes overwhelm you. Andrea Stephens counsels
you on handling major sources of stress, including school,
dating, money matters, self-image, and more. Now you
can beat stress before it burns you out!

Tough Turf by **Bill Sanders**
In these pages, Bill Sanders reveals the secret to believing
in yourself. You can be assured that no matter where you
come from...what you look like...or how popular you are
...you've got what it takes to be a winner!

Great books for building your relationship with God:

Goalposts: Devotions for Guys by **Bill Sanders**
Hot Trax: Devotions for Guys by **Ken Abraham**
Outtakes: Devotions for Guys by **Bill Sanders**
Graffiti: Devotions for Guys by **J. David Schmidt**

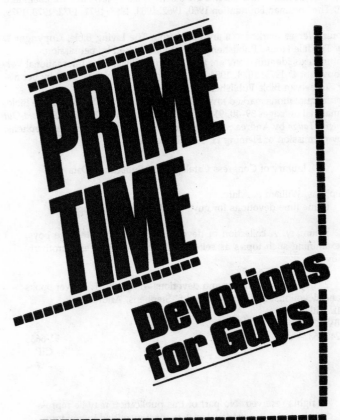

PRIME TIME

Devotions for Guys

Bill and Andrea Stephens

Fleming H. Revell
A Division of Baker Book House
Grand Rapids, Michigan 49506

Scripture quotations marked NAS are taken from the New American Standard Bible, © The Lockman Foundation 1960, 1962, 1963, 1968, 1971, 1972, 1973, 1975, 1977.

Scripture verses marked TLB are taken from The Living Bible, Copyright © 1971 by Tyndale House Publishers, Wheaton, Ill. Used by permission.

Scripture texts identified NIV are from the Holy Bible, New International Version, copyright © 1973, 1978, 1984 International Bible Society. Used by permission of Zondervan Bible Publishers.

Scripture quotations marked KJV are from the King James Version of the Bible.

The material on pages 39–40, 91–92, 128–129, and 161–162 is from *Stressed-Out But Hangin' Tough* by Andrea Stephens, copyright © 1989 by Andrea Stephens. Used by permission of Fleming H. Revell Company.

Library of Congress Cataloging-in-Publication Data

Stephens, William A., date.
　　Prime time devotions for guys / Bill and Andrea Stephens.
　　　　p.　cm.
　　Summary: A collection of devotional readings for teenage boys, examining such topics as self-image, stress, dating, and brotherly love.
　　ISBN 0-8007-5391-7
　　1. Boys—Prayer-books and devotions—English. [1. Prayer books and devotions. 2. Christian life.] I. Stephens, Andrea.
II. Title.
BV4855.S74　1991
242'.632—dc20

91-6638
CIP
AC

Copyright © 1991 by Bill and Andrea Stephens
Published by Fleming H. Revell
a division of Baker Book House Company
P.O. Box 6287, Grand Rapids, MI 49516-6287

ISBN: 0-8007-5391-7

Third printing, January 1993

Printed in the United States of America

To our parents, R. J. and Joanne Ardner, Nell Jean Stephens and the late Bill Stephens. Thank you for your guidance and encouragement in our formative years that we have been able to pass on to other people's kids.

With love,
A&B

A heartfelt thanks to:

Our guest authors and special friends, the Reverend Chuck Legvold, Associate Pastor at First Presbyterian Church, Kokomo, Indiana, and Ted Pierce, Presbyterians for Renewal, Youth Staff Member. We appreciate your willingness to share your guidance with these young men.

The friends who read parts of this manuscript and gave us valuable feedback, especially our teen helper Ralph Hawkins.

Our friend Carol Mulker who once again joyfully typed this manuscript, taking a heavy load off our shoulders and helping us to keep the girls' and guys' books straightened out.

And to our caring family and friends for their much-needed prayer support!

Contents

A Word From the Authors

Read This Before You Begin!

Tons of homework, student council meetings, football practice, girls, trombone lessons, swim meets, youth group, girls, tennis tournaments, FFA Club, band practice, your new job, television, and girls! There are so many things pulling you in different directions, competing for your time. And there are only twenty-four hours in each day. Guys are busy!

Plus, in this teenage time of life, when you are struggling to figure out who you are, it seems everyone has an opinion about everything! Your parents say one thing, your friends say another, your social life is pulling you in one direction, your church in another, some of the music you listen to says to forget God and just please yourself. So many voices! Who are you supposed to listen to? Who can you believe?

That's why, more than ever before, you need to set aside some Prime Time with God. Spending time learning from God's Word and having heart-to-heart prayer time with Jesus will give you the guidance, wisdom, and strength you need to make it in the nineties. So, we wrote this book to help you. We've included the important stuff you need to know.

Here's How to Use It

Pick a time five or six days each week when you are awake and alert to do a short study. We suggest trying to study at the same time each day—before school, after dinner.

Don't do it late at night on your bed when you're ready to fall asleep. Chances are you won't remember a thing the next day!

Each week you will study one topic. Begin each day with prayer, asking God to open your heart and mind to His truth. Now, dig in! Look up the Scriptures. Write your responses. Ask yourself how you can start living out what you're learning. Then, close each day with the suggested prayer including other needs you want to tell God about. Listen intently for God's answers. Watch closely for His hand working in your life.

At the end of the week, review the Scriptures you read each day and pick out your favorite one. Now write it out in the space provided. Challenge yourself to memorize it. Hide it away in your heart. You can do it!

If you start to fall behind in your study, don't quit! Just pick up where you left off or start fresh with a new week. Just do your best and be flexible.

You may find it helpful to share this devotional book with a brother or friend. It can be used for individual or small group study. We recommend that you use a New American Standard or Living Bible to accompany this book. We pray these studies will change your life!

Your friends,
Bill and Andrea Stephens

Run to Win

Do you not know that those who run in a race all run,
but only one receives the prize? Run in such a way
that you may win.

1 Corinthians 9:24 NAS

■■■■■■■■■■■■■■■■■■■■■■■■■■■■■■■■■■■

Greg LeMond has competed in the Tour de France three
times. He has won the famous road race three times. Le-
Mond is a man who rides to win!

According to a newspaper report, LeMond won his first
tour in 1986. He missed the race in 1987 and 1988 because
of a hunting accident that left him seriously injured. In
fact, Greg watched the 1988 race from his hospital bed.
After his recovery, he was determined to get back in
shape. His goal was to compete in the 1989 race. He did.
He won.

This last year, 1990, Greg LeMond once again earned
the prized cup. But it was not easily earned. To compete
and win in a race like the Tour de France, much training,
sharpening of skill, and technique are required. It takes
commitment to your goal!

15

In the eyes of the world, Greg LeMond is a winner. What does it mean to be a winner in the eyes of God?

God's criteria for a winner are much different from most. According to God's scorecard, you don't have to be the best, you don't have to have the most expensive equipment or even the best-rated coach. You just have to have Jesus.

Accepting Jesus into your life gets you started on the Christian race. Through Bible study you learn the rules to this race so you can run effectively. The Holy Spirit is your guide, your personal trainer. Eternal life in heaven with the Lord is your goal! Focus your eyes on the Lord, your example. It won't matter so much if you stumble—no one will run ahead of you because you're running your race yourself. It's just you and God. To Him, because you have chosen to follow His Son and be on His team, you have already won!

> Dear Jesus, teach me how to keep my eyes focused on You as I run this Christian race to win! Amen.

Prime Time This Week

All Christians are in a race. They are running toward their goal—Jesus Christ and eternal life with Him. Paul tells us in this week's Scripture to run our race to win. Don't just hop along the racetrack—get out there and run!

This week you'll uncover some training tips from the Bible, the handbook on life. These Scriptures will help you run with confidence, endurance, and joy!

Monday

First things first! Read 2 Timothy 2:5. If you want to win the prize, you have to compete according to the rules. Don't get disqualified. The Bible is your rule book. Make it a daily habit to read it. You are off to a great start by reading this devotional book. Keep going!

Prime Prayer: Ask Jesus to help you be more committed to your Bible reading, so you'll know the rules to living your Christian life successfully.

Tuesday

Now that you're learning the rules, you'd better find out who it is you are running this race against. It's not other Christians. We're all on the same team! Who is your opponent, your adversary? Find out in Ephesians 6:12, 13 and 1 Peter 5:8. Who is it? What are his goals? _Satan, To make you sin_

_____

_____

_____

Prime Prayer: Ask Jesus to keep you very aware of your opponent so he won't be able to trip you up.

Wednesday

Any good athlete knows that you never turn and look back to see how close the opponent is. Looking back will slow you down! What advice does Paul give in Philippians 3:12–14? Will God lead you to victory? Read 2 Corinthians 2:14. _Paul says that he is not perfect + hasn't learned all he should yet, But he keeps working to be all Christ wants him to be. Yes_

Prime Prayer: Ask Jesus to keep you looking forward—forgetting your past mistakes and moving on. When Satan tries to remind you of your wrongs, tell him to scram!

Thursday

A crooked path is harder to run than a straight one. What running tip does Proverbs 3:5, 6 give to help you get the kinks out of your path? _Put God first. trust the Lord not your self + he will direct you._

Prime Prayer: Ask God to help you trust Him even when you don't understand the situation or why He's leading you in the direction He is. The result? A straight path.

Friday

Here are the secrets to running a good race. To begin, get rid of things that hold you back (bad influences, a lazy attitude), drop off the sin that keeps tripping you up, add patience to your run, fix your eyes and heart on your goal: Jesus Christ. Now, top it off with joy! Jesus' key to enduring His race was knowing the joy of the results! Read all about it in Hebrews 12:1, 2. What is holding you back in your Christian life? What do you keep tripping over? What gets your eyes off Jesus? _Sin, Sin, Sin_

_____

_____

_____

Prime Prayer: Ask God to give you the spiritual power to overcome the things that are messing up your race.

■■■■■■■■■■■■■■■■■■■■■■■■■■■■■■■■■■■

THIS WEEK'S MEMORY VERSE: PICK IT! WRITE IT! REMEMBER IT!

_____

_____

_____

_____

■■■■■■■■■■■■■■■■■■■■■■■■■■■■■■■■■■■

Give Me a Light

Thy word is a lamp to my feet, and a light to my path.
Psalm 119:105 NAS

Have you seen the popular, overplayed Bud Light commercials on TV? I think anyone who ever watches the tube, even for a few minutes, has seen them. The scene is usually of a burly ol' guy demanding a light from a meek-looking, servant-type fellow. So the little guy goes out and brings back a light, any kind of light, just to please the big guy. First he brings a candle, then a torch, a glass chandelier, a blinking neon light! But that's not what the big burly guy wants. He wants a Bud Light. He probably would have gotten what he requested if he'd been more specific. But let's give that little guy a break. He was just trying to do his job. He *did* bring a light. A typical light is something that gets rid of the darkness, and he did return each time with that!

Light is very necessary, no matter what the form. Light helps us see where we're going. If we roam around in the dark, we will get lost and probably trip and fall over something. We need light! In Psalm 119:105, God's Word, the Bible, is called a light. God's Word gives us direction and guidance. When you aren't sure what to do in certain situations, go to the Bible. There you will find helpful words of instruction that will filter through your confusion and shine a clear light on the path God wants you to take. Without the light, you will end up on the wrong road or be doing the wrong thing. You will stumble around in the dark. First Peter 1:25 says that God's Word lasts forever, a solid foundation to build your life on. So, join me as I say "Give me a light—God's light!"

Dear Father, sometimes life is rough and the world is dark out there. I don't always know what I should do. Help me to remember to turn to Your Word so I can clearly see where I'm going. Amen.

Prime Time This Week

This week, discover how God's Word can act as a light that shines on the road God wants you to take. It will help you with tough decisions. Get hold of a Bible concordance where the Scripture verses are listed according to subject. Then, look up the topic you are struggling with and see what God has to say about it. Now follow His well-lit path. The following examples will help you get started. Helpful hint: Memorizing the order of the books of the Bible will help you find Scriptures faster!

Monday

Your parents have warned you against going to drinking parties, but you promised Tim you'd be there. Let Colossians 3:20 make your decision. What does it say?

US children should always obey our parents, for that pleases the Lord.

Prime Prayer: Ask God to help you honor your parents' guidance and His Word.

Tuesday

A classmate just told you some hot gossip. You can't wait till you see Chuck next period. He'll just cringe when he hears this. But wait. Should you really pass it on? Read 2 Timothy 2:16. According to this verse what should you do? Why is this the best decision? How does gossip hurt people? _Stay clear of foolish discussions. Because it is in the Bible. It makes people feel bad, mad, angry_

Prime Prayer: Ask God to help you keep gossip to yourself so it stops with you and stops needless hurt to others.

23

Wednesday

You and a certain girl have never been friends. In fact, because of what has happened in the past, you are enemies. You ignore each other all the time. Check out Matthew 5:43–48. What does Jesus instruct you to do? How would acting lovingly and praying for this girl change your relationship? _Love + pray for enemies_ _because God forgave you. God_ _would help you be friends_ _again_

Prime Prayer: Ask Jesus to give you the willpower and the maturity to love and care for others no matter what they say or do to you.

Thursday

Your brother is very sick and needs you to fill in on his paper route. Getting out of bed at 5:00 A.M. sounds horrible. Read and apply Philippians 2:4 to the situation. What would God want you to do? _Do it + with_ _a good attitude. Do unto others_ _as you would have them do unto_ _you._

Prime Prayer: Ask God to keep you from always putting your own desires first and to help you learn to be concerned about others' needs.

Friday

You are so worried about flunking your math test, your best friend being mad at you, and your grandmother in the hospital, that you aren't even thinking about the Lord! Look up Philippians 4:6–9. What can you do and how can God help? _You can pray, he will help you with your test + grandma, but you have to do your part._

_____

Prime Prayer: Ask God to forgive you for forgetting to turn to Him the very times when you need Him most.

▪▪▪▪▪▪▪▪▪▪▪▪▪▪▪▪▪▪▪▪▪▪▪▪▪▪▪▪▪▪▪▪

THIS WEEK'S MEMORY VERSE: PICK IT! WRITE IT! REMEMBER IT!

_____

_____

_____

_____

_____

▪▪▪▪▪▪▪▪▪▪▪▪▪▪▪▪▪▪▪▪▪▪▪▪▪▪▪▪▪▪▪▪

Prime Topic:
SELF-IMAGE

Guest Author: Charles C. Legvold

Take Another Look

Look at the birds of the air; they do not sow or reap or store away in barns, and yet your heavenly Father feeds them. Are you not much more valuable than they?

Matthew 6:26 NIV

■■■

Mike's letter, written from college, was upbeat and exciting. His classes were challenging. He was dating a wonderful young lady, and he was involved in a Christian fellowship on campus. Mike was on top of his world.

It was a far cry from his life just a few months earlier, when his world was on top of him, driving him closer and closer to the possibility of taking his own life. As he shared his feelings with me, I thought to myself that I had never seen a young man so full of promise yet with so little hope. Mike's great discouragement came from a disease that had robbed his family of prosperity, his childhood of happiness, his body of strength, and now threatened to rob his eyes of sight. What he saw best, he remarked, was a dead-end future and a premature death—why not just get it over with?

I had learned that the best way to help people in Mike's position was to help them discover something they didn't know about themselves. So I asked Mike to talk about his past accomplishments, his present labors, and his future goals. He mentioned that the great love of his life was landscaping. In fact, he had crafted marvelous yards and gardens all over town, greatly impressing homeowners. He also had a marvelous singing voice, with which he had inspired our church many times. And he was always being called by classmates facing difficulties because they knew what he had gone through. He had been able to help them in most cases.

After he finished, I asked him, "Mike, why is it that you think so little of your life when others think so very much of it?" As he searched for an answer, I added, "And consider how much value you have to God. He sent His Son to provide, through His death, a way for you to have eternal life." And then, almost as if a light had been turned on inside of him, he smiled. He had discovered the importance of seeing himself as others, especially God, saw him. And while it did not take away all of his problems, it did give him the encouragement to live on and live for Christ.

Father, until I met Jesus, I never knew just how much You loved me. Remind me, whenever I am discouraged or low, of the great value You have placed upon me. In Jesus' name. Amen.

Prime Time This Week

Acceptance is a need everyone has. To be liked and loved for who you are helps you to grow and blossom into the person God truly wants you to be. Yet, total and honest acceptance is hard to find. That's why people wear masks. They pretend to be someone they really aren't in hopes of being accepted. If everyone continues to wear a mask, no one will ever really know anyone else. That's why you need to take off your mask. As you show people who you really are, eventually, they will do the same. And it won't really matter if others accept and like everything about you. It's impossible to have everyone you meet like you. We are all different. We can accept others based on their personhood. It's so reassuring to know God doesn't judge us as others do. His love is a big love. He accepts us into His family with open arms.

Monday

The real you, the inner person, is where God desires truth. Read Psalm 51:6. When you are truthful about who you really are, you are being wise. Who in your life do you need to be yourself with? How do you think they'll respond to the real you? _No then, he would ask questions about my life or ignore what I have to say. Maybe, Maybe not._

29

Prime Prayer: Ask God for courage as you start to let others know who you really are, what you think, and what you feel.

Tuesday

Thousands of teens have a lagging self-image because they don't feel good enough. They think they're inadequate. What does God say? Read 2 Corinthians 3:4, 5. As a Christian, where does your adequacy come from? How can God help you measure up? _trusting in God. He will help us be true in what we say._

Prime Prayer: Pray today for God to replace your feelings of inadequacy with His adequacy!

Wednesday

Start today by reading Romans 9:20. What did the clay say to the potter? Have you ever asked God that same question? How does God see you? Read Psalm 139:13, 14. How does this help you appreciate your individual uniqueness? _Why have you made me like this. Yes. Special, God made every thing of us complex, amazing, & different_

Prime Prayer: Ask God to help you see yourself as a one-of-a-kind, irreplaceable treasure because, in His eyes, that *is* what you are!

Thursday

Does your self-image suffer because you don't feel you have a purpose in life? God wants to change that! Read the following verses and record God's purpose for you in each of them: Ephesians 2:10, Colossians 1:10, Matthew 5:16. *No. Helping & teaching others about Christ.*

Prime Prayer: Thank God today for creating you for the purpose of good work for others and for knowing Him.

Friday

God wants you to be your *best* self. How are you being less than your best? What or who is holding you back? God made you just right. Be yourself! *Not telling everyone about Christ. I guess nothing*

Prime Prayer: Ask God to show you how to be your best for Him.

■■■■■■■■■■■■■■■■■■■■■■■■■■■■■■■■■■■■■

THIS WEEK'S MEMORY VERSE: PICK IT! WRITE IT! REMEMBER IT!

_____

_____

_____

_____

_____

■■■■■■■■■■■■■■■■■■■■■■■■■■■■■■■■■■■■■

Get Off My Back!

Many a man proclaims his own loyalty, but who can find a trustworthy man?

Proverbs 20:6 NAS

■■■■■■■■■■■■■■■■■■■■■■■■■■■■■■■■■■■

I hear it all the time. "I hate it when my parents check to see if I'm really at the library or at a friend's. I wish they'd get off my back. They just don't trust me!"

In case you haven't figured it out yet, trust is not automatic. It's earned. I realize that because you are struggling for independence and privacy, parents seem like untrusting detectives. But before you start shouting, "Amen," in agreement, listen to this true story.

Rob had big plans to go to Mark's party on Saturday night. Everybody who was anybody would be there, even Lacey, the cute girl in biology class. Rob was keeping his plans quiet because he knew his parents wouldn't let him go. He didn't drink much, but his folks wouldn't want him anywhere near this group. They were known party animals. Their reputation preceded them! Still, Rob wanted to go. Missing the party would put a huge dent in his social reputation. But, as it goes, the best kept secrets leak out.

Rob's parents heard about the party through the grapevine. His mom called around to see if Mark's parents were going to be home on Saturday evening. Of course, they weren't. In fact, they were out of town and didn't even know about the party.

Just as he thought, Rob's parents forbade him to go. He was steamed. All kinds of hateful things ran through his mind about his mom and dad. But on Sunday afternoon, when he heard the scoop about Mark's party, Rob felt a twinge of gratefulness toward his folks.

The party had been wet and wild, but also wicked and life-wrecking. The noise of drunk kids and the distinct smell of pot came from Mark's house. A neighbor called the police, and most of the kids were in trouble big time! Arrests were made, parents were called. It was a mess. Worst of all, Rob heard that Lessa, his friend from choir, had gotten really wasted and a couple of jerks took advantage of her. Rob's heart was broken for Lessa.

Rob's heart was also glad he was not at the party. Even though he had spent Saturday evening feeling cheated, on Sunday he was secretly grateful that his parents cared enough to not let him go to Mark's party. Rob also knew that to regain his parents' trust, he would have to be up front with them, telling the truth about his whereabouts and being wise enough to stay away from questionable situations like Mark's party.

Dear Jesus, I am starting to understand that my parents need and want to trust me. Teach me to remember that the next time they check up on me. Most important, teach me to be trustworthy, to always tell the truth about where I'm going so they won't feel the need to check me out. Thank You. Amen.

Prime Time This Week

Your parents' trust is cut-and-dried. If you lie to them, you lose their trust. If you tell them the truth, you gain their trust. I know teens who purposely lie to their parents. How about you? Do your parents trust you? If so, keep up the good work. Or, have you lost their valuable trust? Let's look at how to gain it back.

Monday

Proverbs 3:3 (TLB) tells you to never forget to be truthful. It is a virtue to hold tightly and keep deep within your heart. Do you value truth? How do you feel when others are truthful with you? Be honest. _yes, good_
(like them more

Prime Prayer: Ask God to help you be a truthful person and to be thankful when others are truthful with you.

Tuesday

The fastest way to regain parents' trust is this: Stop lying. Read Colossians 3:9. It plainly states it! What happens when you lie, then have to lie to cover that lie, and on and on? _You dig yourself a bigger & bigger hole that you can't get out of_

Prime Prayer: Pray that when you feel the need to lie, God will help you through the situation because you chose to be honest instead.

Wednesday

Read John 8:44 to find out who is the originator or father of lies. He will tempt you to lie. Submit yourself to God each day to stay away from the temptation to lie. So, when you're tempted to fib, who is behind it? _Satan_

Prime Prayer: Pray that you'll recognize Satan trying to encourage you to lie and then that you'll choose not to, because you want to follow God.

Thursday

Read James 3:1–12. What small part of your body can cause big problems? Are there hurtful words you have said to your parents that you need to take back? Practice holding your tongue and guarding your words. How will this help in your relationships with others?

tough   keep it good

Prime Prayer: Ask God to help you be consistent so that there is not evil and good coming out of your mouth, only good.

Friday

Do your friends lie to their parents? Your folks will be quick to pick up on this. Be careful of the influence your friends can have on you. Read 1 Corinthians 15:33. What would happen if you and your friends made a pact to be honest in all situations? (Remember, the *facts* are always your friend.) _Then you would always be honest_

Prime Prayer: Ask God to help you be a positive influence on your friends, but if it's not working, then ask for the courage to get new friends.

■■■■■■■■■■■■■■■■■■■■■■■■■■■■■■■■■

THIS WEEK'S MEMORY VERSE: PICK IT! WRITE IT! REMEMBER IT!

_____

_____

_____

_____

_____

■■■■■■■■■■■■■■■■■■■■■■■■■■■■■■■■■

Stress Stuff

Thou wilt keep him in perfect peace, whose mind is
stayed on thee: because he trusteth in thee.

Isaiah 26:3 KJV

■■■■■■■■■■■■■■■■■■■■■■■■■■■■■■■■■■■■

Stress. It has become so common in the eighties and
nineties that it's accepted as a normal part of life. In fact,
it's practically fashionable. Stressed-out is the way to be.
Or is it? Do any of these situations sound familiar to
you?

Gary wasn't reacting very well to the news. His brain
was completely crowded with the worst possible thoughts.
*Are the other kids at school going to make fun of me? Will I ever
live this one down?* Gary's teachers and parents had
decided—Gary was to be held back a year in school. All of
his friends would go on to high school. Not Gary. His
tangled thoughts were making it even harder to pay attention during class. Great. That, of course, made the situation worse because he was getting even further behind
at school.

Andy held several track records at his high school. He was good in many events, especially high hurdles. But today's meet didn't go so well. Andy's grandfather is in the hospital recovering from a major heart attack. Andy was thinking about all the times his grandfather had taken him fishing and quail hunting. Plus he always came to Andy's track meets. But not today. Andy approached the hurdles as usual but accidentally hit the tops of two hurdles, sending them to the ground. He could hardly believe it. Andy's worry over his grandfather's heart attack was affecting his physical coordination. His track events turned out miserably.

It's afternoon now. Mark is home from school. He finished his homework early and doesn't have much else going on. Nothing good on TV. He doesn't want to read. He fidgets around with his younger brother's kickball for a while, then kicks it into the garage. Feeling restless and having nothing else to do, Mark decides to get something to eat. He really can't put his finger on it, but he feels anxious. Why?

Gary, Andy, and Mark are stressed-out! Stress is the feeling you get when you get tense, worried, uptight, and feel little control over your life. You long for inner calmness or peace. But how do you get it? The triumphant technique that worked in *The Karate Kid* will work for you . . . FOCUS!

When you are feeling stressed, where do you focus your thoughts? On the problem, or on the Lord? Isaiah 26:3 offers the key to stomping out stress: Focus your thoughts on the Lord and He will give you the peace you need to make it through your tough times. School, parents, girls, a job—whatever is stressin' you, hand it over to the Lord. Trust Him to work it out for good. Then you will feel His peace gently fill you.

Dear Jesus, when life gets tough and even when it's not, keep my thoughts on You so the strength of Your peace will keep me going. You, Jesus, are the Prince of Peace. Be the Prince of my heart. Amen.

Prime Time This Week

The stress you experience in your life usually starts in your mind, in your thoughts. Your thoughts can cause or calm your worries. Thoughts can give you ulcers or take them away. Control your thoughts and you'll control your stress. Inner peace and lack of stress is directly linked to your mind, according to Isaiah 26:3. Let's see how you can focus, fix, and glue your thoughts on the Lord so His peace will replace your stress.

Monday

Trust is a vital ingredient in stress reduction. After you pray, do doubtful thoughts and questions fill your mind? Trust the Lord! Stop worrying! Read Romans 8:28. How does this verse help you to trust the Lord and His plan for your life? _he said he will work good in your life if you love him_

> *Prime Prayer:* Ask God to continually remind you that He is in control of your life, working out every detail. He is dependable and can be trusted!

Tuesday

We already know that thoughts affect your stress level. Well, exactly what kind of thoughts are you supposed to have that will lessen stress? Read Philippians 4:8, 9. List here the things you are to think about. When you think on these things, what does verse 9 promise you will receive in return? _pure, good thoughts_

> *Prime Prayer:* Ask Jesus to help you keep your thoughts on what is pure, good, positive, and in line with His Word. Now make an honest effort to do it!

Wednesday

Are you afraid God doesn't know what you're thinking about? Do you think He is unaware of your needs? If so, tell Him everything! In exchange for your troubles and worries, His peace will guard your _____ and your _____ . Find out in Philippians 4:6, 7.

> *Prime Prayer:* After you tell God your thoughts, ask Him to surround or guard your heart and mind with His peace, keeping doubtful thoughts far away.

Thursday

Don't let negative thoughts enter your mind. Chase them away whenever they try to sneak in. Talk positive to yourself and watch how your stress level goes down, down, down! Write three positive statements about a situation that is troubling you. ___*If I work*___ ___*I will get money. Be satisfick.*___ ___*Obey.*___ _____

> *Prime Prayer:* Ask God to help you keep the thoughts you think in the silence of your mind very positive and very trusting toward Him.

Friday

All teens struggle with stress. But stress is just a warning signal that says there is something else going on that you're trying to cope with! That's why I wrote an entire book on the subject. My book *Stressed-Out, But Hangin' Tough* is devoted to helping you identify and cope with the stress in your life. Get a copy today!

> *Prime Prayer:* Ask the Lord to help you identify the situations in your life that are stressing you out now, and hand them over to Him!

■■

THIS WEEK'S MEMORY VERSE: PICK IT! WRITE IT! REMEMBER IT!

_____

_____

_____

_____

■■

What a Faithful God!

The Lord's lovingkindnesses indeed never cease, for His compassions never fail. They are new every morning; great is Thy faithfulness.

Lamentations 3:22, 23 NAS

Our God is a faithful God! The Bible tells over and over of the faithfulness of our Lord. For instance: He is faithful to forgive our sins when we ask, to protect His children from Satan, to preserve us, to be loving and compassionate toward us, to help us escape temptation, and to keep all the promises in the Bible! (Check these out yourself: 1 John 1:9, 2 Thessalonians 3:3, Psalm 31:23, Lamentations 3:22, 1 Corinthians 10:13, Hebrews 10:23.)

What exactly does it mean to be faithful? It means to be dedicated or committed to a person or cause. It's to be loyal, trustworthy, and to follow through, that is, doing what you say you're going to do. God is truly faithful to

His children. He is a loyal and dedicated friend. Can you think of a particular situation when God proved faithful to you? It doesn't have to be a big thing, God is faithful in small ways, too.

God has been faithful to me in so many ways. He has always provided me with a job so I wouldn't go hungry or homeless. When my old car finally went to "car heaven," God helped me figure out a way to afford a new one. When I needed several suits for my new job, the Lord directed me to a store that had the exact size and style I needed and at one-third the cost of regular suits!

I appreciate God's dedication to me, but I was not really aware of His commitment to me until I became committed to Him. Faithfulness is a two-way street! As God is faithful to us, we respond out of gratefulness, and in return we are faithful to Him.

How can you, as a teenage Christian, be faithful to the Lord? Well, by being loving and kind to others, keeping the commandments, praying, and reading your Bible. By discovering and doing God's will for your life and choosing to stay away from things that are questionable or evil. When you are faithful and committed to the Lord, He is faithful and committed to you. Faithful! It's a great road to be on.

Dear Lord Jesus, Your Word tells me of so many ways You are faithful to me. Help me to recognize Your dedication to me and in turn may I be motivated to be faithful to You. Amen.

Prime Time This Week

God is faithful to His children. When you recognize His faithfulness to you, it encourages you to be faithful to Him. You are motivated by His love and loyalty. Therefore, faithfulness goes both ways. This week you'll discover how God is faithful to you and how you can be faithful to Him. Being faithful and loyal takes determination and effort. It's not always easy, but it's always worth it!

Monday

See for yourself how God promised to be faithful. Ready for some page turning? Look up all the Scriptures listed in the first paragraph of this devotion. How does reading about God's faithful track record make you feel? _safe_

_____

_____

_____

Prime Prayer: Ask God to show you all the ways in which He has been faithful to you and thank Him for each one.

Tuesday

Are we to keep God's faithfulness to ourselves, like a big secret? Read Psalm 89:1 to find out. How does telling others about God's faithfulness help your faith and theirs to grow? _It m ite save them, God will praise you._

Prime Prayer: Ask God to keep you mindful of the ways He has been faithful to you, so that you will be eager to tell others.

Wednesday

Read Proverbs 28:20. When you personally choose to be faithful to God, does He ignore you, taking your dedication to Him for granted? Does He bless your faithfulness? _no /yes_

Prime Prayer: Praise God for His loving response to your faithfulness.

Thursday

The parable of the talents in Matthew 25:14–30 is really a test of faithfulness. What happened to the servant who didn't faithfully use his gifts or talents for the Lord? Which

servant do you want to be like? _____ he was thrown
out, The won w/ 5 vs bags
of mony

Prime Prayer: Ask God to help you be faithful to Him
in small ways and in large ways, so that He will some-
day say to you, "Well done, my good and faithful
servant."

Friday

Faithfulness is important in all of our relationships. Who
are other people in your life who have been faithful to
you? Who have you been faithful to? Faithfulness is a
quality that builds better families and friendships. _____

_____

_____

_____

Prime Prayer: Ask God to help you develop more
faithfulness in your relationships so they will be more
meaningful and fulfilling.

■■■■■■■■■■■■■■■■■■■■■■■■■■■■■■■■■■■■■

THIS WEEK'S MEMORY VERSE: PICK IT! WRITE IT! REMEMBER IT!

_____

_____

_____

_____

_____

■■■■■■■■■■■■■■■■■■■■■■■■■■■■■■■■■■■■■

Guest Author: Ted Pierce

Earthballs and Enemies

You have heard that it was said, "Love your neighbor and hate your enemy." But I tell you: Love your enemies and pray for those who persecute you, that you may be sons of your Father in heaven. . . .

Matthew 5:43–45 NIV

■■■

No one in our eighth grade class liked Bobby. We had all come to the conclusion that Bobby was a smart-mouth, know-it-all punk who needed to be taught a few lessons in proper junior high social skills. After Bobby learned these lessons, then maybe, I would be his friend. All I had to do was wait for the perfect time to teach Bobby some of these lessons.

The time arrived one day during gym class. As usual, Bobby was causing trouble. Today it happened to be with one of my best friends. Out of the corner of my eye I saw Bobby had pulled my friend into a viselike headlock. I rushed over and demanded that Bobby release my friend or else! Bobby just laughed in my face. I quickly proceeded to double my fist, cock back my arm, and fire an explosive punch into his stomach. Bobby, with no air left in his entire body, keeled over and hit the floor with tears rushing from his eyes. My friend and I ran off and waited for gym class to start.

When the gym teacher found out what my friend and I had done, he had a lesson for *us!* He explained that punching, ignoring, and teasing Bobby was no way to help make friends, just enemies. To help us remember this lesson, he had us blow up an eight-foot earthball that was needed for his next class. My friend and I spent forty-five minutes trying to blow up that huge earthball with our tiny lungs! That was one dizzy forty-five-minute lesson I will never forget.

Jesus also had a few things to say about the way we treat others. He lived in a society that, much like ours, taught men the way to treat an enemy. We are taught to use hate, violence, fighting, and even destruction. Jesus taught a totally different message. He said we are not only to love and pray for our friends but also our enemies and those who persecute us. For a young man to be a "son of our Father," he will have to practice loving enemies and praying for those who persecute him and others. Trying to live a life like the one that Jesus taught and practiced means loving and praying for those we do not particularly like or who do not like us. Punching someone in the stomach or ignoring or teasing him is the way the world treats an enemy, not the way a Christian should.

Dear Lord God, help me to love those people who are hard to love. Help me to be an example of one who loves and cares for others. Amen.

Prime Time This Week

It doesn't matter how hard you try, there will always be people in your life who don't like you. Maybe it's something you've said or done, maybe it's not. For some guys, it's just the fact that you are better at sports, have nice clothes, make better grades, drive a car to school, have a girlfriend, have more hair on your chest, or whatever! They just decide to not like you. They make themselves your enemies and set themselves against you. Enemies are a fact of life. Jesus knew that. That's why He talks to us about enemies and how He wants us to treat them. What we choose to say and do to others is important to God. This week, let's look at what Jesus has to say about loving your enemies and those who mistreat you.

Monday

Can you believe it? Luke 6:27, 28 actually tells you to pray for your enemies! Why? Because prayer helps to change your attitude toward your enemy and hopefully change your enemy's attitude toward you. Who knows? You may end up being friends! What other two things does this Scripture say to do? _____

_____

_____

_____

> *Prime Prayer:* Ask the Lord to give you love and understanding toward your enemies so you will be willing to pray, bless, and do good to them.

Tuesday

Enemies often do things that make you want to get revenge. But God says don't! Read Romans 12:19–21 and Matthew 5:39, 40. How are you supposed to treat an enemy? _____

_____

_____

_____

> *Prime Prayer:* Ask God to help you have a giving and patient attitude toward those who persecute you and make your life rough.

Wednesday

Will your loving response to enemy fire be rewarded? How does God treat evil people? Read Luke 6:34–36 to find out. Write the answers here. _____

_____

_____

_____

Prime Prayer: Thank God for rewarding you when you treat mean people with kindness, just as He does.

Thursday

Check out Matthew 7:12. This verse is also known as the "Golden Rule." It is golden because it's a valuable lesson! Is there someone you have been mistreating? Are *you* being an enemy to some guy at school? How could applying this verse make you change the way you treat him? _____

_____

_____

_____

Prime Prayer: Ask Jesus to open your eyes to the way you treat others, helping you to care for them like He does.

Friday

Make a list of those who may be your enemies or who you dislike. Begin the habit of praying for them this week. Be sure to include that mean teacher or school bully. _____

_____

_____

_____

Prime Prayer: Ask the Lord to remind you to focus on moving these people from your foe list to your friend list.

■■■■■■■■■■■■■■■■■■■■■■■■■■■■■■■■■■■■

THIS WEEK'S MEMORY VERSE: PICK IT! WRITE IT! REMEMBER IT!

_____

_____

_____

_____

_____

■■■■■■■■■■■■■■■■■■■■■■■■■■■■■■■■■■■■

The Right Combination

I am the way, and the truth, and the life; no one comes to the Father, but through Me.

John 14:6 NAS

■ ■

It's only the second day of your sophomore year and you're already late. Nevertheless, you absolutely must stop at your locker before your first class to get your algebra book. You've successfully dodged the other rushing bodies. There it is. Your new locker, number 406. You start to turn the dial on the lock when it happens. BRAIN FADE! You can't remember the combination. Was it 29–15–3 or 3–29–15? Maybe it wasn't 29 at all. You try 15–3–26. No luck. The tardy bell blares in the hallway. Great! You don't have the right combination. You frantically pull on the dial, talk to it sweetly, then threaten to bash it in. Nothing works.

Without the right combination, you can't get into your locker. Likewise, without the right combination, you can't get into heaven, either! That's what combination locks and heaven have in common. You need to know how to get in or you'll be left standing there dumbfounded. It doesn't count to *think* you know how to get in. You have to know for sure.

If I asked you that famous question, "If you died today, would you go to heaven?" how would you answer? Some people would say they've tried to be good, or they gave money to the poor, or they sang in the youth choir, or they visited the old folks' home at Christmas. Maybe they think that owning a Bible or going to church will guarantee their entrance to heaven. None of these are the right combination! Why just hope you'll go to heaven when you can know for sure?

The Bible holds the key. It tells us exactly how to get in those pearly gates of heaven. Here it is! Turn the dial a full circle to the left and stop at John 14:6. Jesus says no one can get to the Father, who's in heaven, except through Him. We need to believe in Jesus to get into heaven. We also need to acknowledge our sins and our need for God. We *need* to know we need Him! Now turn the dial to the right, stopping at Romans 10:9, which tells us that if we say Jesus is our Lord and believe in our hearts that God raised Him from the dead, we will be saved. Saved from hell, that is.

Okay, the final turn. Slowly direct the dial back to the left, stopping at Ephesians 1:13. Here we're told that after we believe in Jesus and accept Him as our Savior, our entrance to heaven is sealed by the Holy Spirit who comes to live in us. There it is. The right combination! Try it for yourself right now. Be sure you're going to heaven. Don't wait. You never know when that tardy bell will ring! Believe in Jesus, His death and resurrection, and the Holy Spirit in you. CLICK. The lock falls off, the door swings open, you're in!

Heavenly Father, thank You for making it so clear how to get into heaven to spend forever with You. I'm so grateful to know the door to heaven will never be closed to me, because I have Jesus in my heart. Help me to share the right combination with my family and friends. Amen.

Prime Time This Week

Jesus is so awesome! He is your key that unlocks heaven's door. He is your SAVIOR. But He's so much more than that! Jesus wants to be your Lord and your friend. He becomes your Lord when you obey His commandments and trust Him with your life. He won't lead you astray. He loves you. He becomes your friend when you open up and let Him in on your life's day-to-day happenings. You develop a personal relationship with Him. You become best friends, buddies, pals. It's a whole new life! So much better than when you were standing on the other side of His door, locked out! This week you'll learn more about salvation and your new friend, Jesus!

Monday

Now you know the right combination to spend eternity in heaven. But, don't get confused! Salvation is a gift, an act of grace and love on God's part. You don't have to *earn* it, but just accept it through faith. (It's believing!) Read Ephesians 2:8. Did you have some mixed-up ideas about how to get to heaven? Write them here. _____

_____

_____

_____

Prime Prayer: Thank God for setting you straight and giving you the gift of salvation.

Tuesday

When you have Jesus in your heart, things start to change! Why? Because you've become new on the inside! God's Spirit is in you! Read 2 Corinthians 5:17. What old habits or beliefs in your life do you need to get rid of now that you are in Christ? What new things have happened in your heart since you became a Christian?

_____

_____

_____

_____

Prime Prayer: Ask God to help you shrug off your old self and put on the love and morality of Jesus each day.

Wednesday

Heaven is the eternal home of all Christians. What will it be like? Read Revelation 21. What does verse 4 say there will *not* be in heaven? How do verses 11–23 describe the appearance of the Holy City? _____

_____

_____

_____

Prime Prayer: Thank God today that His heaven will be a beautiful place without tears and pain, just pleasure from being in His presence.

Thursday

What happens to people who don't accept Christ's salvation? They are eternally separated from God, in hell. How does Revelation 21:8 describe it? _____

_____

_____

_____

Prime Prayer: Ask God to help you share about Jesus to others so they will spend eternity in heaven, too.

Friday

Abraham from the Old Testament was called God's friend. Read Isaiah 41:8 and James 2:23. Why was he God's friend? Because he obeyed and honored God. Read John 15:13–16. Jesus describes how we become His friends. What does He say (verse 14)? How can you become better friends with Jesus? _____

_____

_____

_____

Prime Prayer: Ask Jesus to help you be a better friend to Him by doing what He wants you to do and by spending time in His Word.

■■■■■■■■■■■■■■■■■■■■■■■■■■■■■■■■■■■

THIS WEEK'S MEMORY VERSE: PICK IT! WRITE IT! REMEMBER IT!

_____

_____

_____

_____

_____

■■■■■■■■■■■■■■■■■■■■■■■■■■■■■■■■■■■

Being Put on Hold!

Wait for the Lord; be strong, and let your heart take courage; yes, wait for the Lord.

Psalm 27:14 NAS

■■■■■■■■■■■■■■■■■■■■■■■■■■■■■■■■■■

Randy slammed his bedroom door. Why in the world did he have to get Jim and Margaret for parents? How could they be so unreasonable? "Every normal kid in the world gets his driver's license at age sixteen," he shouted out from his bedside. "They just can't do this to me," he kept saying over and over again. Waiting another whole year seemed totally unfair! Those 365 days would take forever. Yet, what could he do? He dreaded the idea of putting his driver's license on hold. He had no choice but to face the humiliating thought of riding the school bus one more year.

Randy hated waiting! He despised the long lines at the video store, sitting in a traffic jam, and friends who were always late. Maybe he was a little impatient, as others said, but in his mind this waiting until age seventeen to drive was cruel and senseless. Then, he remembered the story of Jacob from last week's Sunday school lessons. Jacob knew what it was like to wait for something he wanted.

Jacob had fallen in love with the most beautiful girl he had ever seen. Her name was Rachel. He could tell she also loved him. Her father, Laban, agreed that Jacob could marry his daughter, but only if he agreed to work for Laban for seven years first! Since Jacob was so in love with Rachel he consented. When the seven long years of hard work and waiting were finally up, Laban went back on his word to Jacob and gave him his other daughter, Leah, instead. Jacob was very angry because he had waited so long for Rachel. Laban again promised Jacob that he could have Rachel, but only if he would work for him for seven more years! Because Jacob loved Rachel so much, he gave in to Laban's requirement.

As Randy remembered, God was teaching Jacob that when you love someone you are willing to wait for them. Randy knew God was saying that because he loved his parents he should be willing to wait for his driver's license. Randy didn't have to agree with his parents' decision, but now, he could accept it. He felt his anger toward his parents dissolving. One more year on the bus wouldn't kill him, he thought to himself as he opened his bedroom door to go back downstairs. In fact, it's a lot better than fourteen years!

Sometimes God's answer for us is not yes or no, but "wait." While these waiting times are never easy, we can wait with the assurance that God's timing is always perfect, even when God speaks through your mom and dad!

Dear heavenly Father, help me to trust You enough to wait for Your perfect timing in my life. Thank You for loving me and for having a plan for my life. Give me the patience I will need for the waiting times. Amen.

Prime Time This Week

Why is waiting so hard? Probably because we're the kind of people who want everything right now! Instantly. Waiting isn't comfortable. It makes us feel put out. But how many times have you rushed ahead and done something, and it didn't work out as well as if you had patiently waited? This week discover the importance of waiting on the Lord!

Monday

Isaiah 40:31 is the famous "waiting" passage. What does it teach about the benefits of waiting for the Lord's timing in your life? How is renewed strength an absolute necessity in learning to wait? _____

_____

_____

_____

Prime Prayer: Ask God to renew your weary feelings as you wait upon Him to work in the situations you face.

Tuesday

In Luke 24:49 and Acts 1:4, 5 Jesus instructed the disciples to "wait here." Why? Because God was going to do something special! If we don't wait, how can we mess up God's plans for us? _____

_____

_____

_____

Prime Prayer: Pray that you will be more patient, waiting on God's special plans.

Wednesday

One of the benefits of waiting for the Lord's leading, instead of rushing out to do your own thing, is found in Psalm 37:34. How will having honor with God be an asset in your life? _____

_____

_____

_____

Prime Prayer: Ask God to help you wait on His timing so He'll honor you and so that you will honor Him!

Thursday

When we are waiting on God to answer our prayers, should we be uptight, pacing our rooms, worried about others who are getting ahead of us? How should we behave? Find out in Psalm 37:7–9 and Philippians 4:6.

_____

_____

_____

_____

Prime Prayer: Ask God to help you focus on Him, to trust Him, and to know He'll supply our needs.

Friday

God told Abraham He would make him the father of many with his wife, Sarah. But Abraham's wife continually didn't conceive. So instead of waiting for the Lord's perfect timing, Sarah urged Abraham to conceive a son with her maidservant Hagar. Read Genesis 16:1–4, then 17:15–21. Did God accept Ishmael as Abraham's chosen son? How do you think Abraham and Sarah's

impatience affected Hagar and Ishmael? It's always better
to wait! _____

_____

_____

_____

Prime Prayer: Pray that you won't jump ahead of
God's perfect plan, but wait on God.

■■■■■■■■■■■■■■■■■■■■■■■■■■■■■■■■■■

THIS WEEK'S MEMORY VERSE: PICK IT! WRITE IT! REMEMBER IT!

_____

_____

_____

_____

_____

■■■■■■■■■■■■■■■■■■■■■■■■■■■■■■■■■■

Praise . . . Just Do It!

Let everything alive give praises to the Lord! You praise him! Hallelujah!

Psalm 150:6 TLB

■■■■■■■■■■■■■■■■■■■■■■■■■■■■■■■■■■■

When you were a little kid, did you ever attend Vacation Bible School at your church? Can you remember singing your heart out on "Jesus Loves Me" or "Praise Him" or "Father, I Adore You"? Little kids are so free to sing and clap and praise the Lord. Their hearts are pure; their motives are right.

Then they grow up. Ooo. They become teenagers. Too cool to show they love God, too afraid of what others might think of it. Trying to get a group of 13- to 16-year-olds to sing love songs to Jesus is like trying to land a seaplane in the sand. No way! But why? Are others really more valuable than the Lord?

Every year millions of teens attend rock concerts, waving their hands in the air to their music stars. In a sense, they are praising them. Even Christian teens find themselves idolizing these artists who really are anti-Christ in their beliefs. Yet, they can't seem to get into praising the very One who loves them, saves them, and is the key to their often troubled lives. Well, what about praising the "true rock," Jesus Christ?

Psalm 150:6 says that everything that is alive or is breathing gives praise to the Lord. Pinch yourself! Are you alive? Great! You qualify. God wants *YOU* to praise Him!

Why should you praise the Lord? Glad you asked. Praising the Lord helps you focus in on Him. That allows your problems and troubles to drift away, putting your trials in perspective. Praising God gives you new strength, courage, and hope. Praise also makes you feel closer to God and more aware of His presence in your life. In fact, the Bible tells us that God inhabits, or lives, in the praises of His people. When you praise God, He is right there with you! Praising the Lord benefits you, His child, but it also makes His heart glad. Take some quiet time alone. Praise God for all the blessings He has given you. Praise Him for what He has done, praise Him because He is Lord. Praise Him. Just do it!

Dear Lord, You alone are worthy of my praise and adoration. Help me to feel less self-conscious about praising You, thanking You, and loving You. You mean so much to me. Amen.

Prime Time This Week

Let's get practical. Exactly *how* do you praise the Lord? The Bible says to make a joyful noise to Him. Lots of definitions could fit "joyful noise." Your voice doesn't have to be perfectly on key or tuned up with the guy next to you. The Bible just says to sing—croak, if you want—just make it happy! And loud! Now add a few instruments if you want. Psalm 150 lists all kinds to use: guitar, trombones, cymbals, drums, organ, flute, and so on! You can stand, sit, kneel, raise your hands or clap them. Want to do it alone? No problem. Buy a praise tape and cut loose!

Monday

God works in our lives daily! It's proper to praise Him for things He does. Jesus and King David did. Read Matthew 11:25. What did Jesus praise God for? Now check out Psalm 40:1–3. David praised God for what? Now flip over to John 17:4. Jesus said that He glorified God on earth by doing what? How could you glorify God today? _____

_____

_____

_____

Prime Prayer: Ask God to open your eyes to all the things He does for you every day and praise Him for each of them.

Tuesday

Praise can actually release God's power to work in our lives. Praising God is the life source to our Christian faith. Read Acts 2:46, 47. The Lord saved people and added to the number of Christians because the people did what? Do you need God to do something in your life? Pray and praise! Watch what happens. _____

_____

_____

Prime Prayer: Tell the Lord about the situation facing you, then praise Him to allow His power to work through you.

Wednesday

Shout and dance praises to the Lord? You've got to be kidding! No, really! Praise can be quiet and reverent, but praise sessions in the Bible weren't like that! Read Psalm 66:1 and Psalm 98:4–6. How would you describe the noise level? Check out the movement level! Read Psalm 149:3 and Psalm 150:4. Be footloose for Jesus. Let His joy take over! If your church doesn't praise like this, ask why? Then have your own private praise party!

_____

_____

_____

_____

> *Prime Prayer:* Ask Jesus to show you how to get filled with His joy and to shout, sing, and dance your praises to Him. Don't be shy!

Thursday

What does it mean to sacrifice something? Right. It means to give it up. Read Hebrews 13:15. How would you offer up a sacrifice of praise? What makes it a sacrifice? Because at first you may not *feel* like doing it, but you do it anyway, because it pleases God. How do you feel about praise? _____

_____

_____

_____

> *Prime Prayer:* Ask the Lord to teach you to praise whether you feel like it or not, knowing it will lighten your heart and His.

Friday

Whistle a happy tune! Sing a praise to Jesus! James 5:13 says singing is the sign of a cheerful person. Actually it works both ways. You can sing praises because you *are* cheerful or to *get* cheerful. Remember, Satan hates praise! It's the perfect way to keep Satan off your back and out of your life. Practice praise today. How do you feel afterwards? _____

_____

_____

_____

Prime Prayer: Ask God to help you remember that praising Him will cheer up your day.

■■

THIS WEEK'S MEMORY VERSE: PICK IT! WRITE IT!
REMEMBER IT!

_____

_____

_____

_____

_____

■■

Uptown Girl

Don't be teamed with those who do not love the Lord,
for what do the people of God have in common with
the people of sin? How can light live with darkness?

2 Corinthians 6:14 TLB

■■■■■■■■■■■■■■■■■■■■■■■■■■■■■■■■■■■■■■■

Brian was in love. Her name was Emily and she was
fine. Emily had long blonde hair that curled around her
shoulders. Her creamy skin, clear blue eyes, and moist
lips sent a chill up Brian's spine every time he was near
her. And luckily for him, that was quite often.

Brian finally asked Emily on a date after months of prod-
ding from his friends. Brian just didn't think she'd say
yes. After all, Emily was from a wealthy family. She
dressed great, smelled great, and looked great in her red
convertible. Brian and Emily had been dating now for
three months. They liked playing tennis together, riding
horses, and getting Chinese food! It seemed like everything was going along smoothly. Everything except one
thing. Brian was a Christian, Emily was not. It was causing them more and more problems. Because Emily was

rich and popular, she insisted on being seen at all the hot parties. She didn't see the harm in getting wasted and even kissing other guys. She said it meant nothing. Plus, she teased Brian about going to church on Sundays—especially on Saturday nights when she was trying to entice him with her charm.

Brian had given in to Emily a few times, but he was unhappy. This just wasn't working out.

What's the harm in just dating a non-Christian? you may ask. Let me explain. When you start spending lots of time with someone, you may become romantically and emotionally attached. It's very hard to keep a clear head when your feelings are involved. You may enjoy each other's company, but when it comes to discussing meaningful issues, you won't agree. Your values and viewpoints will be different. You won't have much in common. And breaking up is hard to do! (Just ask Brian.)

That's exactly the point of 2 Corinthians 6:14, 15. Christians and non-Christians are different. It's like oil and water. You can put them in the same jar, shake them vigorously, but within seconds they start to separate. No matter how hard or how long you shake, they just don't mix.

So, no matter how wonderful the girl is, find out if she values Christ and the Christian life-style as much as you.

> Dear Lord, it's so easy to get swept into a relationship with a girl who's so gorgeous. But help me to take a good hard look at who I date—her values and beliefs—before I get too attached. Amen.

Prime Time This Week

This dating stuff is tricky business! One day the girl says, "Hi!" the next, she ignores you. One day you're tight and madly in love, the next, you meet your cousin's gorgeous friend and you're out of there! Dating is like a hammock swing. It isn't super sturdy, which makes it sort of challenging to get on and off, but when you're on there swinging away it's fun. But watch it—when those limbs that hammock is tied to break, there you are, flat on your rear end! Love is a crazy thing. But your teen years are a good time to test the dating waters. Find out what you do and don't like in a girl. It helps you prepare for the Big M: Marriage! Yes, that's *way* down the road! This week you'll take a closer look at the bumps and potholes you'll face on that Lover's Lane.

Monday

What qualities do you look for in a girl? Be selective. Just because she's a *female* and shows interest doesn't mean she's the one for you. This week's Scripture is loud and clear. Make sure she's a Christian (and not saying she's one just because you want her to!). Read the famous verses on love in 1 Corinthians 13:4–8. What qualities does it suggest your woman should have? (Notice it says nothing about looks!) _____

_____

_____

_____

Prime Prayer: Ask the Lord to help you keep your heart and eyes open to a girl with scriptural qualities.

Tuesday

Do your parents approve of the girl you like? Remember what Ephesians 6:1, 2 say? Look it up! To honor your mom and dad means to respect their opinion. You may not be able to see straight through your dreamy eyes, but your folks can sense things—they may be better judges of character! What problems does it cause to date a girl your parents don't like? _____

_____

_____

Prime Prayer: Ask God to help you honor your parents, even in your dating life.

Wednesday

Dating can often get too serious too fast. That's why group dating is better than one-on-one. It keeps the conversation light and the hormones in check! If your body insists on being alone, watch out! Keep sex a part of Health Education class, not a Saturday-night event. Design four group dates. What could you do? Where could you go? Now, you'll have ideas handy! _____

_____

_____

_____

Prime Prayer: Ask God to let you see the value, safety, and fun of group dating. Now, be willing to be the one who suggests group activities!

Thursday

The big breakup. Rejection. Definitely a pothole on the dating path! Read Psalm 34:18. Where is God when your heart's breaking? How can He help you? _____

_____

_____

_____

Prime Prayer: Ask God to help you forgive and forget, knowing that the right person for you may take years to find.

Friday

Girls and guys are total opposites. He says yes, she says no! It's a big problem in relationships today, yet God *made* us opposites! We're not alike. That's so we'll balance each other. Yet, common interests are important. What interests do you value that you want your girl to share? _____

_____

_____

_____

Prime Prayer: Ask God to help you see that opposite can be good!

■■■■■■■■■■■■■■■■■■■■■■■■■■■■■■■■■■■■■

THIS WEEK'S MEMORY VERSE: PICK IT! WRITE IT! REMEMBER IT!

_____

_____

_____

_____

_____

■■■■■■■■■■■■■■■■■■■■■■■■■■■■■■■■■■■

New Kids on the Block

Do not merely look out for your own personal interests, but also for the interests of others.

Philippians 2:4 NAS

■ ■

They're the hottest group in town. The heartthrob of America. The biggest appeal since the Beatles. Like them or not, the New Kids on the Block are at the top!

The fame, the money, the fans, the music—it keeps a teen group pumped. Sure, it's a natural high for a while, a real charge. But all popularity has its price.

As reported by *People* magazine (August 13, 1990), the New Kids' fame can take its toll. "At home, I cannot walk down my own little street," says Jordan Knight. He also reported that on tour even the hallway of the hotel was off-limits. "Some days it gets to me pretty bad," says he. Popularity can be an intrusion of privacy. You're restricted, people watch you closely, and they usually have a comment to make about everything you do.

Jordan also reported that he felt lucky there are five group members, saying that it would be too hard to handle if there were just one. "Thank God we have each other."

Popularity is a strange thing. It seems like everybody wants it, but once you've got it, you don't know what to do with it. To be popular means you get lots of attention. Yet, popular kids often admit they are lonely.

They may have a lot of friends, but they don't have any true friends. The strength and support a person gets from a small group or network of close friends is far better than being liked and lifted up by lots of people.

Many teen stars struggle with these problems. Danny Ponce, who plays Willie on "The Hogan Family," told *TV Guide*, "I just graduated from high school with all my credits. The sad thing is, I didn't know one person at my graduation."

Kirk Cameron, five-year star of *Growing Pains*, has kept his life and head together. His secret? He says that you just have to be yourself.

Jesus was very popular in His day. But when it got right down to it, He had only a handful of true friends. Being loved by the crowd is not as meaningful as being loved by a few who care and are there for you.

> Dear Lord, the appeal of popularity entices me, but I see that developing a small group of close friends is where it's at. Help me to be a good friend and to value my friendships. Amen.

Prime Time This Week

Sometimes there is no rhyme or reason for a person's popularity or lack of it. Some kids are popular because of their personality or talents—it comes naturally. Other teens strive for popularity, actually compromising themselves for the sake of acceptance and votes from others. Is getting trapped in the popularity game really worth it? Consider this week's Scripture studies before you answer.

Monday

Popularity itself is not wrong, but it can get people in trouble if they abuse it or if they gain it with the wrong motive. Some guys *work* to get popular, their motive is selfish. They step on and put down the "little guys" to climb higher up Popularity Mountain themselves. This kind of popularity usually crashes in due time. Read James 3:16. What goes hand in hand with this kind of selfish popularity? What evil things have you witnessed in these kinds of people? _____

_____

_____

_____

Prime Prayer: Ask God to keep you from wanting popularity for selfish reasons and pray for the people you know who fit this mold.

Tuesday

Many popular people are self-promoters. They are always telling you how great they are, what new thing they own, and what cruel trick they played on someone. They are against God, who doesn't want us to act that way. Read Philippians 2:3, 4. What attitude are you to have? Who are you to consider important? Are you to look out for only your own interests? _____

_____

_____

_____

Prime Prayer: Ask God to make you into the unselfish kind of person He wants you to be.

Wednesday

Michael W. Smith sings a song about Joshua 1:1–8 called "Be Strong and Courageous." Read those verses. God told Joshua that he would be successful and popular if he would read, study, and apply God's Word. Joshua obeyed. Now read Joshua 6:27. Was Joshua popular? Yes! And for the right reasons—he honored and obeyed God! Do you want to be strong and courageous against the pressure to give in to the ways of the "in" crowd? What changes do you need to make in your life to put God's command to Joshua into effect? _____

_____

_____

_____

_____

Prime Prayer: Ask God to help you devote yourself to His Word so you will know what you're to do and you will be popular with God!

Thursday

Compromising costs a lot. There's a price to pay! Have you used any of these reasons to compromise: "If I don't do it, I won't fit in, then I won't have any friends." "Everyone else does it!" When we deny ourselves to please others, we hurt the way we feel about ourselves because we aren't being true to what we know is right. When you compromise, you stop being yourself! Read Proverbs

16:25. What ways have you or a friend taken for the sake of popularity that ended up backfiring? _____

_____

_____

_____

_____

Prime Prayer: Ask God to help you be yourself and not to compromise for popularity's sake.

Friday

Wanting to be liked and having a few close friends is the need of every human being. Knowing and being truly known by a handful of people you can trust is far better than worldwide fame. Jesus showed us this style of friendship through His intimate relationship with His disciples. The crowd pushed in around Him and demanded His attention, but it was His few close friends who stuck by Him. With whom in your life could you develop this close and caring relationship? In what ways would this kind of friendship be rewarding for you? _____

_____

_____

_____

_____

Prime Prayer: Ask the Lord to open your eyes to some guys or a brother with whom you could be true friends. Then pray for courage to be yourself and let that person know you.

■ ■■■■■■■■■■■■■■■■■■■■■■■■■■■■■■■■■■■ ■

THIS WEEK'S MEMORY VERSE: PICK IT! WRITE IT! REMEMBER IT!

_____

_____

_____

_____

_____

■■■■■■■■■■■■■■■■■■■■■■■■■■■■■■■■■■■■■■

God's Guaranteed Success

> This book of the law shall not depart from your mouth, but you shall meditate on it day and night, so that you may be careful to do according to all that is written in it; for then you will make your way prosperous, and then you will have success.
>
> Joshua 1:8 NAS

■■■

Go to your local bookstore and you will find the shelves packed with books filled with advice on how to be successful! Of course, whether a person is successful or not all depends on how they define the word *success*. Here is what a few teens had to say:

Patti told me, "I think I will feel successful if I am happy. It doesn't matter to me what I am doing or how much money I am making, but if I am smiling, I'm a success."

Jason felt this way: "My dad owns his own company. He is a very successful businessman and quite respected in our city. Following in his footsteps, I feel I had better make something of myself or it will make my dad look like he didn't raise me very well. I do want to make him proud of me."

Mike's viewpoint was: "Success is when all the bills are paid, you have a little extra money for the movies, but most important, you have success when your life is straight with God. If I screw up my life in every other area, it won't matter. My relationship to God is what matters most."

Patti, Jason, and Mike have different ways of measuring their future success. The amount of success they each experience will depend on whether or not they live up to their own standards.

The world's view of success is to be in control, wealthy, educated, good-looking, and put yourself first. God's view is different. He doesn't pressure us to be millionaires or professors. He challenges us to follow Him. Following Him, we will find success.

Joshua 1:8 (NAS) describes God's formula for success. The interesting fact about this verse is that when we obey the Lord and live at peace with Him, He makes us prosperous by supplying all our needs and gives us a heart of love and joy. Our success can spread to every area of our life when we let the Lord in and follow His Word!

> Dear Jesus, my true desire is to keep my eyes on You and Your Word, because in obedience to You I will have true success—both inside and outside. Amen.

Prime Time This Week

Once you're out of high school or college and into the work world, the pressure to succeed stares you in the face. At least you may feel that it does. Friends are watching. Employers are watching. Parents are watching. The thought of failing terrifies many teens as they look to their future. As a teen you can learn right now what God's formula for success is! Let's study the ingredients of the awesome recipe this week.

Monday

Joshua 1:8 says that prosperity comes from what? To meditate means to think deeply about something over and over. Reading, studying, and memorizing. Hiding God's Word in your heart will light your path and direct you toward success. But just knowing God's Word is not enough. What does Psalm 119:105, 106 (TLB) say you must do? _____

_____

_____

_____

Prime Prayer: Ask the Lord to give you the desire and the diligence to study and meditate on His Word, but most important, to obey it.

Tuesday

God told Joshua he would be successful if he meditated on the Word both day and night. In the morning and in the evening! Why is this such a key factor in God's plan for success? Why day and night? Read Proverbs 8:17 (KJV) and then Psalm 16:7. _____

_____

_____

_____

Prime Prayer: Ask God to help you make time in your schedule each morning and each evening to read His Word so that you may find Him and hear from Him even as you sleep.

Wednesday

Some people think you've become great and successful in life when you have others working under you or for you. Errand boys! Is it true? Are you to serve or be served? Find out in Matthew 20:26–28. Why do people who have "servant attitudes" usually have more friends? How do your friends and family respond when you do things for them? _____

_____

_____

_____

Prime Prayer: Ask God to give you a servant's heart and to help you start today to do things for others, putting them first and yourself second.

Thursday

According to Psalm 1:1–4, what are the key ingredients to prosperity? How does listening to evil and associating with the ungodly or a non-Christian ruin a person's success? _____

_____

_____

_____

Prime Prayer: Ask God to make you aware of the ungodly counsel in your life so you can get rid of it and listen only to the wisdom of His people. Also, delight in God's laws so you, too, will be like a fruitful tree.

Friday

Success and prosperity are more than money and fame. Success in a Christian's life is about honoring God and living a life pleasing to Him. It's also about inner success—having a heart filled with love, joy, peace, and contentment! How is inner success even more important to God than financial success? _____

_____

_____

_____

Prime Prayer: Ask God to help you live a life more pleasing to Him so that your life will reflect inner success and you will be a true witness of God's love in your life.

■■■■■■■■■■■■■■■■■■■■■■■■■■■■■■■■■■■■

THIS WEEK'S MEMORY VERSE: PICK IT! WRITE IT! REMEMBER IT!

_____

_____

_____

_____

_____

■■■■■■■■■■■■■■■■■■■■■■■■■■■■■■■■■■■■

A Cloudy View

But if we confess our sins to him, he can be depended on to forgive us and to cleanse us from every wrong.

1 John 1:9 TLB

■■■■■■■■■■■■■■■■■■■■■■■■■■■■■■■■■■■■■■

Kevin was excited about his family's move to the East Coast. He finally said good-bye to all his friends. The next day he would be headed to a new town, a new school, new friends, and a new house. Kevin's parents had purchased a house two months ago when his dad first learned of his transfer. Kevin could hardly wait. He was going to have his own room this time, and he could make it look any way he wanted. Kevin's dad's description of the new house was beyond Kevin's hopes. A big white house, a porch swing, a swimming pool, a stone fireplace, a game room. And it was only a few blocks from his new school. For two months the house sat waiting for Kevin and his family.

Kevin was a bit disenchanted when they pulled up to the house in their jam-packed station wagon. Because the house had sat so long, the yard was overgrown, and the house looked dirty—especially the windows. The wind, rain, and hot sun had done a number on what was once clear glass.

When he got inside, Kevin was even more bothered by those dusty, stained, and spotted windows. He couldn't see clearly through them. The view was cloudy, almost like it was out of focus. Kevin decided the first thing he had to do was clean his bedroom windows!

Did you know sin makes our hearts look just like those dirty windows? Sin spots and stains our hearts, often making us want to turn from God because we sense we are unclean. Sin also clouds our outlook on life. It makes us focus on our shortcomings and our failures, making us feel that we can't live up to God's expectations.

Yet, sin can also make us more intently aware of our need for God and the loving forgiveness He offers to us. When we confess our sins to the Lord, the Bible says He will forgive us. He will wash us white as snow, and He'll even forget what we did. God will wash the dirty windows of our hearts and make us clean once again! The best way to keep your heart's window spick-and-span is to wash it every day. Every night before you go to sleep, mentally run through the day's activities. Did you disobey your folks, tell a little white lie to your teacher, purposely forget to return your friend's tape because you didn't want to buy it yourself? Are there, in fact, things you did wrong that you need to tell the Lord about and ask His forgiveness? Do it right then. Wake up each morning with the "Son" shining brightly in your heart.

Dear Lord, sometimes my sins seem so great that I feel separated from You. My vision gets cloudy. I don't understand how You can love me. Yet, when I fall at Your feet asking forgiveness of all my wrongs, You promise to cleanse me. Thank You, Lord, for washing me white as new fallen snow. Amen.

Prime Time This Week

Scripture tells us that everyone has sinned and fallen short of God's glory. Because of our sinful state, God had to send Jesus to die for us. He paid the penalty of our sin! When we accept Jesus as Lord and Savior, through Him our sins are forgiven. Becoming a Christian doesn't mean you'll never sin again. You may, but your aim is to be obedient. That's why we have Jesus. This week let's see what else you can learn about sin and how to stay away from it.

Monday

How does sin occur? James 1:14, 15 says it starts with a temptation that leads to lust (uncontrolled desire), which then leads you to sin. Quench the fire while it's still a flicker! Get rid of your temptations and you'll get rid of sin! Think back and write an example of how something you did wrong started with a temptation that you gave in to. _____

_____

_____

_____

Prime Prayer: Pray that you'll recognize temptation for what it is and that God will give you the strength to say no right then, before the flicker of temptation becomes the fire of sin.

Tuesday

Read Isaiah 59:2. Sin separates us from God. Sin is evil and God is Holy. They are opposites! See Psalm 5:4. Confessed sin brings you back into fellowship with your heavenly Father. Do you keep stumbling over the same sin? What is it? Read Hebrews 12:1. What does it tell you to do?

_____

_____

_____

_____

Prime Prayer: Pray to remember to confess your sins instantly so your relationship with God can be restored, then get rid of whatever keeps tripping you up.

Wednesday

The Psalmist was not afraid to come before the Lord and ask God to reveal his sin to himself and then cleanse his heart. Read Psalm 51:10 and Psalm 139:23, 24. Remember God is *for* you.

> *Prime Prayer:* Ask God to show you areas in your life that aren't pleasing to Him. Allow Him to cleanse your heart as you confess and turn away from your sin.

Thursday

Why do you feel so rotten when you know you've done wrong? You've been convicted! But, by who? Read Proverbs 20:27 and John 16:8, 9. How does the Holy Spirit help you stay on track? _____

_____

_____

_____

> *Prime Prayer:* Ask the Holy Spirit to keep doing His job so you'll stay on the right track!

Friday

Read Romans 6:5 through 8:17. What does it teach you about sin? Now check out Galatians 5:16–25. What is the benefit of walking by the Spirit of God? _____

_____

_____

_____

Prime Prayer: Ask the Lord to give you power over sins as you *choose* to walk by the Spirit and not fulfill the desires of your fleshly, sinful nature.

■■■■■■■■■■■■■■■■■■■■■■■■■■■■■■■■■■■

THIS WEEK'S MEMORY VERSE: PICK IT! WRITE IT! REMEMBER IT!

_____

_____

_____

_____

_____

■■■■■■■■■■■■■■■■■■■■■■■■■■■■■■■■■■■

What a Guy!

What is desirable in a man is his kindness, and it is better to be a poor man than a liar.

Proverbs 19:22 NAS

■■■■■■■■■■■■■■■■■■■■■■■■■■■■■■■■■■■

Have you ever checked out the guys on the cover of *GQ Magazine?* Square chins, straight noses, prominent cheekbones, clear skin, bushy eyebrows, well-built, just to name a few of their high points. Supposedly these kinds of guys are the epitome of men. They are totally male. Hunks. The longing of any sane female.

Oh, really?

I hate to burst their bubble, but it's just not true. And speaking as a female and a former model, I know! Physical attractiveness in a male comes second to the type of guy he is. Proverbs 19:22 says it best. A guy who is caring, loving, kind, sincere, and honest is far more attractive than the insensitive, rude type.

In fact, Jesus was a kind and honest man. The Bible says He wasn't physically attractive to the point that anyone would notice Him (Isaiah 53:2). So why was it that Jesus was the most popular man of His time? Why were people attracted to Him?

Because He cared for them. He was kind. He was gentle. He cared when they were hungry or sick or alone. He was honest with them. He made them aware of who He was and told them the truth about Himself, His Father, and the Kingdom of God. He loved them. That's what made Jesus so attractive.

Deep down, the same is still true. The inner qualities and characteristics of a man make him really attractive. Not his wallet, not his macho look, not his muscles, not his brains. True attractiveness is found in the attitudes and kindnesses of his heart.

> Dear Lord, it seems like the best-looking or richest guys get all the girls. Help me to understand how shallow that scene is and that it's developing my inner person to be like You that will make me an attractive man. Amen.

Prime Time This Week

The old saying, "You can attract more flies with honey than you can with vinegar," is so true! But you can attract a lot more than just flies! A kind and honest attitude can attract more friends, jobs, dates, respect, and a better relationship with your parents. How attractive are your present attitudes? Are they sweet like honey or sour like vinegar? This week's study will let you know about some attitudes you can and can't live without.

Monday

The Bible's criteria for a church leader are some of the very characteristics and attitudes God desires all men to acquire. Read 1 Timothy 3:1–12 and Titus 1:6–9. List them here. _____

_____

_____

_____

Prime Prayer: Pray, asking God specifically to help you develop the godly attitudes He desires in you.

Tuesday

Proverbs 6:16–19 list seven things that God hates! They are things that are not attractive on any man. Read them and list them. How do these seven things cause negative problems in a guy's life? _____

_____

_____

_____

Prime Prayer: Ask God to help you to run from the things that He detests, striving to do what pleases Him.

Wednesday

The world of advertising tries to make a guy feel as though he just doesn't measure up without certain products or clothes. What gimmicks do the media use to try to convince guys the macho look with muscle mass is where it's at? According to 2 Corinthians 4:16, is your inner man or outer man eternally important? _____

_____

_____

_____

Prime Prayer: Ask God to help you realize the man you are on the inside is far more meaningful and long lasting than your looks.

Thursday

Some guys think that getting into fights and arguments with other guys makes them look tough and appealing. The Bible doesn't agree! Read Proverbs 20:3 (TLB) to find out how God sees the fighter. List two good ways to stay out of a fight. _____

_____

_____

_____

Prime Prayer: Ask the Lord to help you keep from looking foolish by staying out of fights.

Friday

The more time you spend with Jesus in prayer, and the more you learn from the Bible, the more attractive your attitudes and outlook on life will be. Read David's prayer in Psalm 27:4. What three requests did he make? How will these three things make a man more appealing? _____

_____

_____

_____

Prime Prayer: Pray that when others look at you they will see the loving and kind reflection of Jesus in you.

■■■■■■■■■■■■■■■■■■■■■■■■■■■■■■■■■■■■

THIS WEEK'S MEMORY VERSE: PICK IT! WRITE IT! REMEMBER IT!

_____

_____

_____

_____

_____

■■■■■■■■■■■■■■■■■■■■■■■■■■■■■■■■■■■■

"Lifestyles of the Rich and Famous"

For the love of money is the first step toward all kinds of sin. Some people have even turned away from God because of their love for it, and as a result have pierced themselves with many sorrows.

1 Timothy 6:10 TLB

■■■■■■■■■■■■■■■■■■■■■■■■■■■■■■■■■■■■■■

All right, I confess. Many times while flipping through the television channels, I've gotten stuck on the exquisitely gorgeous homes and habits shown off by Robin Leach on "Lifestyles of the Rich and Famous." Though the tastes of the stars range from antique lamps to crystal chandeliers, mansions with imported tile pools to dusty horse ranches, you'll always see a captivating display of unique possessions. A single half-hour show can leave the average person feeling like a poor and unknown nobody who lives in a hut, swims in a puddle, and drives a motorized heap of metal with wheels.

Yet, as I think back, I don't ever recall hearing any of

those big stars with big bucks give credit or honor to God on television for the talents they have that earned them the money to buy the things they own.

It is very common for people who start earning lots of money to make money more important than God in their lives. They don't have time or room in their lives for Jesus. They love money, not God who owns all the world and its possessions.

Loving money not only turns people away from God, but it makes them competitive, selfish, and prideful. All of these can lead to sin, causing further separation from God.

The rich and famous, however, will often be the first to admit that after years of chasing careers and money, they're unhappy. You see, having the biggest house, the fastest car, the fanciest clothes does not satisfy a person's inner hunger. Only a personal relationship with God's Son, Jesus, can do that. When I was modeling for the Wilhelmina Modeling Agency in New York, I met many rich and famous people. One actor in particular comes to my mind. He had wealth and worldwide fame, but he was still searching for the real meaning in life. I still pray for him, hoping he will turn his heart toward God.

Being rich and famous isn't all it's cracked up to be. Psalm 37:16 suggests it is much better to have a little money and be a Christian than to own much and be ungodly. I agree.

> Dear Lord, I can see that it's far better to keep You as number one in my life. Keep me from idolizing what others own and teach me to be grateful for what You've graciously given me. Amen.

Prime Time This Week

Thousands of people have sacrificed precious and often irreplaceable things to get the best job, invest in the hottest deal, whatever it takes to get the almighty dollar. Families have suffered because of a workaholic parent or one who travels a lot to earn bonuses. Many families have split up because of money arguments. Worse yet, people, especially teens, who have sensed a lack of money, have gone so far as to steal to get it. Money becomes a god to many people. Loving money ruins people. The Bible offers wise advice about money matters. Take heed.

Monday

Many people are like the man Jesus talks about in Luke 12:15–21. Their lives are spent building bigger houses and buying fancier cars, and so on. What warning does Jesus give these people? What does it mean to be rich toward God? Also read 1 Timothy 6:17–19. _____

_____

_____

Prime Prayer: Pray today for wealthy people who are focused on themselves that they will have a changed heart, be willing to share, be generous, and use their money for others.

Tuesday

Do you have some favorite things that you treasure? Or maybe some special times that you hold dear in your heart? Read Luke 12:34 and Matthew 6:19–21. What kind of things could be treasures that can be kept in heaven?

_____

_____

_____

_____

Prime Prayer: Ask the Lord to help you store up treasures in heaven like your salvation, leading someone to Christ, helping others, and loving your family.

Wednesday

Most people believe that if they are generous and give away money, they'll run out! God says that's not true. Read Proverbs 11:25 and 2 Corinthians 9:6–11. Remember to sow means to give. What is the best attitude to have about giving? _____

_____

_____

_____

Prime Prayer: Ask Jesus to teach you to give so He can bless you even more, plus to help you have a cheerful attitude about sharing.

Thursday

Read Hebrews 13:5. Are you content with what you have? Do you want more and better items? Do you constantly ask your parents for money or new clothes? Do you need to work on your attitude of gratitude? Does this verse imply that having Jesus is better than all else?

_____

_____

_____

Prime Prayer: Ask God to help you see that in Him you have everything because He makes you happy on the inside. Pray to be content and thankful for what you have.

Friday

Here's a toughy for most people. God asks you to tithe from the money you earn whether it's from a job or your allowance. To tithe means to give God 10 percent of the total amount. So, if you earn ten dollars, God gets one.

Get it? Now read Proverbs 3:9–10 and Malachi 3:10. What does God promise for your obedience to tithing? _____

_____

_____

_____

> *Prime Prayer:* Ask the Lord to help you understand that a portion of the money you earn goes to Him as a way of furthering the work of the church and also as a way to thank Him for helping you earn it in the first place!

■■■■■■■■■■■■■■■■■■■■■■■■■■■■■■■■■■■■■■■

THIS WEEK'S MEMORY VERSE: PICK IT! WRITE IT! REMEMBER IT!

_____

_____

_____

_____

_____

■■■■■■■■■■■■■■■■■■■■■■■■■■■■■■■■■■■■■■■

Trick or Treat

And no wonder, for even Satan disguises himself as an angel of light. Therefore it is not surprising if his servants also disguise themselves as servants of righteousness; whose end shall be according to their deeds.

2 Corinthians 11:14, 15 NAS

■■■■■■■■■■■■■■■■■■■■■■■■■■■■■■■■■■■■

My husband recently had the privilege of delivering the junior sermon for the children in our church. He held up a brown paper sack then slowly pulled out a plate of fresh made, hot, ready-to-eat donut holes. The kids oohed and aahed. A sugary sweet donut hole—the perfect Sunday morning snack and a great reward for coming to church. *That Pastor Bill*, they thought, *what a nice guy to bring us donut holes.*

Before giving each child a donut, Bill asked for a volunteer to test them. Hands went shooting into the air. A lucky young boy was selected. As his teeth sunk deep into the donut, his tongue got a good taste of what appeared to be sugar. YUCK! It was salt!

The salty donut hole looked exactly like the sweet sugary ones. The treat turned out to be a trick.

Second Corinthians 11:14, 15 tell of a similar situation where what looks like a treat is really a trick. Satan and his servants make themselves out to look like God's angels and servants. They wear a disguise, hoping you can't tell the difference. Through the years, subtle, deceptive, so-called "churches" and "organizations" have fooled people into believing they are Christian groups when really their underlying motive is to lead people away from Christ. The same can be true of situations. It looks safe enough on the surface, but underneath there's trouble.

For instance, you may think going to certain rock concerts, a quiet beer party, getting some "illegal" help on a test, a secret date with a girl your parents dislike are all tasty little treats. But watch out! They may backfire in your face and turn out to be ugly tricks of the enemy.

God does not trick His children. He does not need to wear a disguise to make Himself look like someone He's not. He is trustworthy. Your heavenly Father wants you to know Him, so you won't ever confuse a treat of His with a trick of Satan.

> Oh, Father, help me to keep my eyes open and my heart focused on You so that I won't be led astray by Satan's tricky tactics. Amen.

Prime Time This Week

An army will never win the war if they don't know who their enemy is or how he works. What are his tactics? His favorite moves? As a member of the Army of God, you must be able to recognize your enemy: Satan. He's not a funny-looking guy in a red suit with horns, a pointed tail, and pitchfork! He is real, alive, and roaming around planet earth! Be wise to him. Take your blinders off and see him for who he really is. He works through others, trying to lead people away from Christ. Study up. God doesn't want you to be ignorant!

Monday

Exactly what is Satan's goal here on earth? Read John 10:10. Satan wants to destroy the Kingdom of God and the lives of Christians. Why? He is absolutely 100 percent evil! Read Psalm 97:10 and Psalm 34:13, 14. How does God feel about evil and our participation with it?

_____

_____

_____

_____

Prime Prayer: Ask God to help you recognize evil and to stay far away from it by drawing closer to Him.

Tuesday

Satan has always been in a power struggle with God. Read the description of Satan's selfish desire to be better than God. Notice each sentence begins with "I will . . ." Find this in Isaiah 14:13, 14. What is it that Satan wants? Remember, God always wins! His Spirit is in us and gives us authority over Satan. See 1 John 4:4. Who is in us and who is in the world? _____

_____

_____

_____

Prime Prayer: Ask God to help you to change your "I will" to "Thy will" and submit yourself to God's authority.

Wednesday

Read 2 Peter 2:1-3. In today's world many musicians have become false teachers, leading teens away from the teachings of Christ. Yet, most teens ignorantly defend their favorite singers. But you can't believe everything you hear! Well, here's how to test their words and their lifestyle. Read 1 John 4:1-3. If the musicians you listen to do not honor God and do not say Jesus is Lord, they are not on God's team. Get hold of Al Menconi's videotape called "Everything You Always Wanted to Know About Rock Music." Don't be fooled. What musicians do you currently listen to? What are the main themes of their songs? Do they honor God? Which group do you think God wants you to quit listening to? _____

_____

_____

_____

Prime Prayer: Ask the Lord to open your eyes to false teaching and eliminate it from your life.

Thursday

Read 1 Thessalonians 2:18. Does Satan try to stop God's plan in *your* life as he did in Paul's? Absolutely! Use your authority over him when he gets in your way, tries to tempt you, or puts evil thoughts in your head. Tell him to leave in the name of Jesus! Read Matthew 4:10, 11. What did Satan do when Jesus told him to get lost? Check out Matthew 6:13. Can Christians ask God to protect them from Satan and his evil plans? _____

_____

_____

_____

Prime Prayer: Ask God to protect you from evil and the evil one! Tell Satan to get lost—you are God's property!

Friday

According to God's Word, the world is black-and-white. People are either for God or against Him. Good or evil. Read Luke 11:23. Who do you know who opposes God?

_____

_____

_____

_____

Prime Prayer: Ask God to open the hearts of your family and friends who need to know Him personally.

■■■■■■■■■■■■■■■■■■■■■■■■■■■■■■■■■■■■■

THIS WEEK'S MEMORY VERSE: PICK IT! WRITE IT! REMEMBER IT!

_____

_____

_____

_____

_____

■■■■■■■■■■■■■■■■■■■■■■■■■■■■■■■■■■■■■

Prime Topic: PRAYER

Guest Author: Charles C. Legvold

Surprised by Results

And the prayer offered in faith will make the sick person well; the Lord will raise him up. . . .

James 5:15 NIV

■ ■

Rob and I were college classmates living in the same dormitory. Since both of us were freshmen, and relatively new Christians, we were learning daily more and more about living out our faith in the power of the Holy Spirit. And as we learned, we agreed to pray with each other daily.

One morning during finals week, right before Christmas, Rob knocked on my door. When I opened it, he looked horrible. He explained that he had been up all night, not studying, but sick, and was afraid that he would miss his final exam that day. Most troublesome to him was a sore throat that did not allow him to even swallow without great pain. He asked me to pray that his sore throat would be healed. My first reaction was to indicate that I had no specific gift in healing the sick and that, maybe, sucking on a throat lozenge might be more beneficial. But he insisted, and so I prayed a very simple prayer: "Lord, I'm not sure I should be doing this, but I'm willing to try. Heal Rob's sore throat so that he can take his test today. In Jesus' name. Amen." I was just about to suggest that he try the lozenge anyway when he got the strangest look on his face. He said, "I just swallowed, and there's no more pain!" Half in amazement and half in joy, we literally danced around the room.

Since that time, I have never hesitated to trust the power of prayer. Nor have I hesitated to pray for someone who was sick. I discovered, much to my own surprise, that prayer has an effect on more than just the person for whom I pray. It also has an impact on me. Every time I pray for someone, it helps the person greatly, often in ways that I do not see. But it also helps *me*; when I see God answer prayer when we turn to Him, my own faith in Him is made stronger. Prayer brings results, both for others and for ourselves.

> Father, never let me forget that You want me
> to bring life and health to others. Instead of
> trusting in my own abilities as I pray, help me
> to trust in what *You* can do. In Jesus' name.
> Amen.

Prime Time This Week

Prayer is one of the privileges we have as Christians. It is a time when we can go to our heavenly Father and tell Him everything that's on our hearts. We can also ask Him for guidance and wisdom in every situation we face. Yet, prayer is more than a privilege, it's a necessity. It's something we *need* to do. It allows us to spend valuable time in God's presence. We build a deeper and more intimate relationship with Him through prayer. It's a time when we can get recharged, renewed, and strengthened to go back out and battle the world. Prayer is also a time when we can learn to surrender our will to the Lord so He can make us willing to accept His perfect answer to our prayers. This week let's see what else we can learn about the privilege and power of prayer.

Monday

When Jesus needed to pray, He went away to a place where He could be alone. Read Matthew 6:5, 6. Where can you be alone with God to pray? Of course, you *can* pray anywhere, anytime. In fact, lots of times during the day you'll find it necessary to send quick "pop-up" prayers to God. Who and what can you pray about? What does it say in Philippians 4:6 and Matthew 5:44? _____

_____

_____

_____

123

Prime Prayer: Ask God to teach you to live in an attitude of prayer, ever ready to come before Him with your needs or needs of others.

Tuesday

Some people think they don't have the right to go to God with their needs. Read Ephesians 3:12. It says that because we have Jesus, Christians have _____ and _____ access (to God) through faith in Jesus! How will knowing this help in your prayer time?

_____

_____

_____

_____

Prime Prayer: Pray that you will better understand God's great love for you and His desire for you to come to Him with confidence.

Wednesday

A sign posted on a church bulletin board read: "A person who kneels before God can stand up to anything!" It's so true! How has prayer made you stronger and more confident? (Hint: It helps to remember what you've prayed for and to expectantly wait for God's answer!) _____

_____

_____

Prime Prayer: Ask God to fill you with strength, courage, and peace as you faithfully make time in your daily schedule to pray.

Thursday

Guess who is praying for *you?* Yes, probably your mom and dad and a friend or two. But who else? Read Hebrews 7:25, Hebrews 9:24, and Romans 8:34. Wow! Jesus makes intercession for us in the presence of God! Intercession means to pray to God on behalf of someone else. Jesus prays for you! How does that make you feel? How does it boost your confidence?

_____

_____

_____

Prime Prayer: Praise God today for Jesus who appears to God on your behalf!

Friday

Prayer is not to be taken lightly. Jesus always prayed to know God's will, for guidance, and for the needs of others. Read Colossians 4:2. What two instructions does this verse give? Now read Colossians 4:3. Prayer changes things! What was Paul asking God to do? Need changes in your life? Pray! _____

_____

_____

_____

Prime Prayer: Ask God to help you devote yourself to prayer, knowing that prayer does make a difference.

▪▪▪▪▪▪▪▪▪▪▪▪▪▪▪▪▪▪▪▪▪▪▪▪▪▪▪▪▪▪▪▪

THIS WEEK'S MEMORY VERSE: PICK IT! WRITE IT! REMEMBER IT!

_____

_____

_____

_____

▪▪▪▪▪▪▪▪▪▪▪▪▪▪▪▪▪▪▪▪▪▪▪▪▪▪▪▪▪▪▪▪

Hey, Lord, Say What?

I was crying to the Lord with my voice, and He answered me from His holy mountain.

Psalm 3:4 NAS

Blake felt frustrated. He prayed and talked to God regularly, but his conversations seemed one-sided. Was God really listening? Did He care about his troubles? Does He really give guidance? Is He still up there?

Hearing from heaven has fascinated people for years. It's especially discouraging to a teen who is making an honest effort at living a Christian life. Blake will be happy to know that the problem isn't that God doesn't answer. It's that too often, we just can't seem to hear Him! There's static on the line. Or perhaps we simply don't recognize God's solution (or don't want to admit that we know what He wants, because it is not what *we* want).

Psalm 3:4 tells us God *does* answer and respond when

we talk to Him. So, how can we hear Him more clearly and recognize His answer? Here's how to clear the line:

1. *The Bible*   Many times the answer or encouragement you need is right in the Bible. As you read, a certain Scripture may suddenly have new meaning. It comes alive. It's just what you needed. That's God.

2. *Other People*   Often God will speak to you through something someone says. It catches your attention and applies to your situation. The person may have no idea he said something that helped you. But when someone shares from wisdom and experience, God uses it as an answer.

3. *Inner Listening*   After you pray, sit quietly and listen for the Lord to speak to you. This won't be an audible voice, but in the form of a thought in your mind, one that you know you didn't think up. If it's positive, good, loving, and in line with the Bible and God's nature, you can trust it. If it's evil or revengeful, it's not God.

4. *Change of Circumstances*   When something that was going wrong suddenly starts working out, or a new option is presented, some call it a coincidence. Well, if it's something you've prayed about, I would call that God. He makes things happen that change our circumstances and answer our prayers.

5. *Follow After Peace*   Another way God can give you direction and answers is through His peace. In the Amplified Bible, Colossians 3:15 says to let God's

peace be the umpire in your life. An umpire is the one who calls the shots and makes the final decisions. When you need an answer to a problem, see which direction you feel peaceful going in. God leads through His peace.

Be on the lookout for the Lord, read your Bible, talk with other Christians, follow after peace, and listen for the Holy Spirit to speak. God does answer prayer. He does not pick and choose whose prayers He will answer. He answers all prayers in the way He sees fit. Trust His wisdom. He loves you. He will answer you. The more time you spend with Him, the more easily you will recognize His voice.

Dear Father, remind me always that You hear when I pray, and that You answer in Your own time, in Your own way. I trust You. Amen.

Prime Time This Week

Every day this week, review and practice the five ways to hear from the Lord. Memorize them so that after you have prayed, you won't walk away and forget about it! Let's look at a few more things that can hinder or help your hot line to heaven.

Monday

In Psalm 5:1–3 David uncovers a great secret. First, he prays in the morning before his day gets into full swing.

129

Then what does he say in verse 3? How does being expectant increase your chances of hearing God's voice?

_____

_____

_____

_____

> *Prime Prayer:* Pray that each day you will be looking
> for God's answer to your prayer, knowing He hears
> you and will respond.

Tuesday

Read Isaiah 59:2. How does unconfessed sin hinder hearing from God? What should you do? Right! Confess your sins to the Lord daily so your .connection will be static-free! _____

_____

_____

_____

> *Prime Prayer:* Ask God each day to forgive your sins
> of the day—list them individually—so your prayers
> won't be hindered.

Wednesday

What is the advice given in Psalm 46:10? How will this information help you tune in and listen to God? _____

_____

_____

_____

> *Prime Prayer:* Ask God to teach you how to be still before Him, chasing all other thoughts away, so you can hear Him speak to you.

Thursday

At the church in Antioch, Paul and fellow believers were gathered together. They were praising the Lord and fasting (skipping a meal for the purpose of prayer), and someone spoke to them. Read Acts 13:1–3. Who spoke to them? Praise put them in the mind-set to hear from the Holy Spirit! List two ways you can praise the Lord during your prayer time. _____

_____

_____

_____

> *Prime Prayer:* Pray to be a praiser because it opens up the way for the Holy Spirit to speak to you.

Friday

Do you have a tough decision to make? Have you ever prayed and then let peace help you make the decision? Read Isaiah 55:12. It confirms that God leads us through His peace. Close your eyes. Take a deep breath. Which option seems like the most peaceful answer to your dilemma? Go with it! _____

_____

_____

_____

Prime Prayer: Pray for God's peace to fill your heart so you know exactly what He wants you to do.

■■

THIS WEEK'S MEMORY VERSE: PICK IT! WRITE IT! REMEMBER IT!

_____

_____

_____

_____

_____

■■■■■■■■■■■■■■■■■■■■■■■■■■■■■■■■■■■■■■■

Majestic Messengers

For he orders his angels to protect you wherever you go.

Psalm 91:11 TLB

■■■■■■■■■■■■■■■■■■■■■■■■■■■■■■■■■■

"I was driving along the road when suddenly I was hit head-on by a truck in the other lane. My head crashed the windshield as my car spun around and landed upside down in a ditch. I remember feeling someone slip their arms around my chest, pulling me out of the car onto the ground. When the ambulance arrived, no one could figure out how I got out of the crashed car. There had been no one around and the truck driver was completely unconscious. I am sure it was an angel who rescued me."

If you heard someone tell a story like this—and maybe you have—how would you respond? Would you think the guy was telling the truth or was totally crazy? What concept do you have of angels? Do you picture them as

133

sweet, kind, cheerful, fantasy do-gooders who float on cotton-candy clouds all day? Do you doubt their existence as some people do, or do you think they are only in heaven, completely unavailable to us, God's children?

I have found most teens have a lot of unanswered questions about God's heavenly host of angels. For instance, does every person really have a guardian angel? What is the purpose of angels? Are they always invisible? Do they talk? Do they have names? Do they fight wars? What do they look like? Are they ranked in any special order? Do they worship God because they have to, or want to? Do they really have wings? On and on. Have you ever asked any of these questions? If so, congratulations! Inquisitive minds want to know. And they'll find out!

If you've been the kind to just blow off the idea of angels, thinking they are make-believe, then get ready! You're about to learn some exciting stuff! For instance, one of the main jobs of God's angels is to watch over and protect you. Angels are available to guard you, keep you from harm. All you have to do is ask God to send the angels to surround you. You also need to be realistic. If you decide to do something ridiculous like dive off the Empire State Building, don't expect a big burly angel to catch you halfway down and softly deliver you to the sidewalk below. Angels protect God's people when they are doing His work and are obedient to His Word.

This week you will be discovering valuable information on angels that will change your view of these majestic creatures.

Dear Lord, open my eyes concerning the truth about angels. Convince me of their reality, so I will confidently call on their assistance. Amen.

Prime Time This Week

Angels! The word itself means messenger of God. That's right! Angels are God's personal messengers. They await God's instruction then fly (yes, they have wings as told in Ezekiel 10:5) off to their destination to deliver a message or to intervene in a situation to protect God's plan from being stopped. Angels are alive and well. Sound unbelievable? Remember who they are working for! With God, all things are possible! Now, let's answer all those questions.

Monday

What is the main purpose of angels? To send messages from God to believers and to minister to God's children. Read Hebrews 1:14, Genesis 28:12, and Revelation 1:1. What was the angel's message to Mary Magdalene in Matthew 28:1–7? Take note: Angels *do* talk and they do appear to people! Check out Hebrews 13:2. _____

_____

_____

_____

Prime Prayer: Pray that you will be more aware of angelic activity and that a kind stranger may be an angel!

Tuesday

Are angels also assigned by God to guard and protect people? What is the answer according to Psalm 34:7 and Exodus 23:20? Now read the story of Daniel's night at "Lions' Den Inn!" What purpose did the angel serve? See Daniel 6:16–23. _____

_____

_____

_____

Prime Prayer: Ask the Lord to help you remember that His protecting angels are there waiting for you to call on them for protection. Each day ask God to send His angels to watch over you.

Wednesday

Do angels fight wars? Yes! They fight against the evil forces of Satan. Read Revelation 12:7–9. Some angels are even known as destroying angels! Read about them in

1 Chronicles 21:15, 16 and Psalm 78:49. How does knowing that God's angels are on your side make you feel? _____

_____

_____

_____

Prime Prayer: Ask God today to send His angels to fight the evil one on your behalf. Now thank Him that powerful angels are on your side!

Thursday

Where do angels live? Read Mark 13:32. Do they have names? Find out in Luke 1:26. Do they freely worship the Lord? See Luke 2:13, 14. _____

_____

_____

_____

Prime Prayer: Ask God to help you be like the angels by praising Him every day and every night.

Friday

Are angels ranked in any special order? Find out about the angel Michael in Daniel 10:13, Jude 9 (*arch* means chief). Do you know any hymns that refer to cherubim and seraphim? Cherubim are angels of the second highest rank and seraphim are the highest order of angels. What do Ezekiel 10:16 and Isaiah 6:2 have to say? _____

_____

_____

_____

Prime Prayer: Spend a few moments thanking God for the new understanding you have of angels and what they mean in the life of a Christian.

■■■■■■■■■■■■■■■■■■■■■■■■■■■■■■■■■■■■■

THIS WEEK'S MEMORY VERSE: PICK IT! WRITE IT! REMEMBER IT!

_____

_____

_____

_____

_____

■■■■■■■■■■■■■■■■■■■■■■■■■■■■■■■■■■■■■

Guest Author: Ted Pierce

Hey, Hey, I Love You

Jesus replied: "Love the Lord your God with all your
heart and with all your soul and with all your mind.
This is the first and greatest commandment."

Matthew 22:37, 38 NIV

■■

Have you ever come home from school and seen the old
black-and-white reruns of "The Andy Griffith Show"? If
you have, maybe you saw one of my favorite characters on
the show, Ernest T. Bass. I still sit back and laugh at the
way he would go crazy when he had a "crush" or would
fall madly in love with a female character on the show.
Ernest T. was a good ol' hillbilly type with old clothes and
no front teeth. He would put all his energy into seeking
out his "woman." He would do wild things like throw
rocks through her window and yell in his country voice,
"Hey, hey, I love you. It's Ernest T. Bass!" He would then
follow his gal around the town of Mayberry and sneak
up behind buildings to scare her, trying to get her

attention any way he could! Ernest T. would stop at nothing to get his woman. He would then pick a fight with the boyfriend of the girl he wanted to date. His entire day and energy would be focused on his dream girl. He could think of nothing else. Ernest T. used all of his simple heart, soul, and mind to try to figure out how to be with the one he loved.

Have you ever had a crush on a girl at school or in your town? Every time you see her, your heart begins to race and your face becomes flushed. You catch yourself doing strange things like following her down the hall, trying to find her locker number, or following her home. (Maybe to throw a love note through her window!) Your inner soul becomes warm if she looks at you, smiles, and simply says, "Hi!" You even find your mind meditating, reflecting, or wandering off with thoughts about this special girl. It may seem as though your entire day and energies are focused on this girl.

The God who created the universe also wants you to use all your energy to seek *Him* with your heart, soul, and mind. God asks you to use your *heart*, the rational and emotional part of your being, to seek Him out. Your heart is where you put things that you hold dear, things that are special and meaningful. That's where God wants to be. Number one in your heart! If your heart races over that special girl at school, how much more does it race as you think of a God who made the world and came down in the form of a man to build a loving relationship with you!

God also desires a relationship with your inner being or *soul*. This means to truly seek God for His will and purpose for your life. God wants to be your highest focus.

Finally, God calls you to use your *mind* in daily meditation, reflection, and thinking. You can educate yourself on the things of God through daily Bible study followed by a quiet time of reflection and prayer. Using our mind to love God also means honoring Him with our thoughts and being a faithful participant in worship. Just like Ernest T. Bass focused all his heart, soul, and mind on the one he loved, Jesus is challenging you to do the same thing with Him.

Dear God, help me to love You with all my heart, soul, and mind. Teach me to focus all my energy on You and to be an example of love to those who surround me. Amen.

Prime Time This Week

What does it mean for you to love God? Certainly you know that God loves *you*. The Bible tells you that God loved you so much He gave up His only Son, Jesus, to die for you so you could have forgiveness of your sins, eternal life in heaven, peace and comfort, even wisdom. Jesus loved you with all He had—with His entire life! That was complete and total love! But how do *you* show love to God? Let's explore that question this week.

Monday

Loving God means making Him number one in your life! That's the point behind our Scripture this week, Matthew 22:37, 38. Putting God first in your heart (loving Him more than your new stereo, favorite car, or musician), first in your desires, and first in your thoughts. List two ways you can personally put God first in each of these areas.

_____

_____

_____

Prime Prayer: Pray that God will show you what people or things you have been putting in front of Him so you can switch it around and make Him number one!

Tuesday

Loving God means loving yourself. That's right. After Jesus told His disciples to love God with their total beings—heart, soul, and mind—He said to love others as they loved themselves (Matthew 22:39). Loving yourself means to have a healthy appreciation for who you are and to respect yourself as a creation and child of God. You have been made in the image and likeness of God Himself. Read it in Genesis 1:26! Don't put yourself down. Don't knock your talents and abilities. How have you been thinking low of yourself? How does loving yourself show you love God? _____

_____

_____

_____

Prime Prayer: Ask God to help you love yourself as He does—through forgiving and accepting eyes.

Wednesday

Loving God means loving others. We show we love God when we reach out to help someone or give them something or pray for them. First John 4:20, 21 puts it to you strong! Read it now and name the people you have been unloving to. Is it a teacher, a classmate, a family member? How can you change and be loving toward them? _____

_____

_____

_____

Prime Prayer: Ask God to forgive you for being rude, mean, or unkind to others. Ask Him to help you show love toward them so you'll be showing love toward God!

Thursday

Loving God means being obedient to His Word. Read John 14:15. It says if you love God, you'll do what? God's commandments are the instructions He gives His children through the Bible. Why do you think that doing

143

your best to do what God asks of you shows that you love Him? _____

_____

_____

_____

Prime Prayer: Ask God to give you the strength and willpower to say no to others and yes to Him, because what you do and say shows that you love Him or you don't!

Friday

Loving God means focusing on Jesus. Read Hebrews 12:1, 2. It says to fix your _____ on Jesus. What happens to the golfer or baseball or basketball player who takes his eyes off the ball? Or the goalie who looks away for a minute or two? What distractions are in your life that cause you to take your eyes off Jesus? What can you do to get rid of them? _____

_____

_____

_____

Prime Prayer: Pray that you will focus your eyes, your attention, your goals, and your time on Jesus so you will win in this Christian race!

■■■■■■■■■■■■■■■■■■■■■■■■■■■■■■■■■■■■■■

THIS WEEK'S MEMORY VERSE: PICK IT! WRITE IT! REMEMBER IT!

_____ _____

_____

_____

_____

_____

■■■■■■■■■■■■■■■■■■■■■■■■■■■■■■■■■■■■■■

NOTE:

THIS WEEK'S MEMORY VERSE: PICK IT! WRITE IT!
REMEMBER IT!

_____

_____

_____

_____

High Five

... And give each other a loving handshake when you meet.

1 Corinthians 16:20 TLB

■■■■■■■■■■■■■■■■■■■■■■■■■■■■■■■■■■■■■■

The big tournament game is over, your team won! The ol' blue-and-gold Tigers did it! They captured the state title. Everybody is so excited they just can't hold back. The players and the faithful fans are slapping high fives, hugging with all their might, giving their hearty handshakes and firm back pats.

Having all witnessed the triumphant trophy taking, the group is united together. They have shared a special experience. And they can't help but reach out and touch!

The early Christian churches were the same way. They shared the unifying experience of seeing and knowing the Lord Jesus. Their lives were changed, they found new purpose, and they were excited. Like a winning team, they were bonded together with joy. In signing off several of his New Testament letters, the Apostle Paul told the

147

early Christians to greet one another with a warm, loving handshake or a holy kiss (cheek-style, I suppose!). This sort of contact showed they were members of the same team, having a caring attitude. But there's more to this reach-out-and-touch stuff.

A friendly handshake, a pat on the back, a high five, or even a quick hug is very comforting and encouraging. It can brighten your day and uplift your spirits. A caring touch says, "Hey, I'm on your side, everything will be all right." Handshakes and hugs can chase away fear, loneliness, and tension, and they are good icebreakers!

The qualifications to be a handshaker or hugger are easy. All you need is a hand, a couple of arms, a willing heart, and someone to hug! Both you and the recipient will be encouraged by the gentle contact of a fellow Christian. Plus, handshakes and hugs can be done anywhere. At church, at school, at the movies, at home. Don't be shy, reach out and touch!

> Dear Lord, how easy it is to offer a hand or a hug to someone. Whether they need a hug or I do, please give me the courage so I can lighten their day and mine. Amen.

Prime Time This Week

Handshakes, high fives, slipping some skin, and hugs are just a few ways to show caring with your hands. Because we see our hands constantly and use them for so many different things, we may take them for granted. But they are really very special and an absolute necessity in our lives. This week we are going to look at various ways the Bible tells us to put our hands to use.

Monday

The Bible's description of the "Proverbs 31 woman" explains three specific uses for hands. Read Proverbs 31:13, 19, 20. For what purposes does she use her hands? As a guy, how can you use your hands for the same useful purposes? Do you like to fix and repair, do yard work, build things, cook? _____

_____

_____

_____

Prime Prayer: Ask the Lord to encourage you to be productive and to put your hands to good use!

Tuesday

There are both positive and negative ways you can use your hands. Negative uses for hands would be punching, slapping, stealing, and making rude gestures. Positive uses would be a gentle touch, hugging, holding hands, a friendly wave, applause, and helping someone. Read Ephesians 4:28. What are the positive and negative uses listed in this verse? _____

_____

_____

_____

> *Prime Prayer:* Pray to be a loving person who isn't afraid to pat a back or hug a friend in public.

Wednesday

It's okay for teens to shake someone's hand when meeting or greeting them. Here's how to shake hands: Sincerely extend your hand to the other person. Grasp their hand firmly, but gently. Don't leave your hand like a "limp noodle" in theirs. A good handshake shows self-confidence and interest in the other person. Do you think a handshake or a high five breaks the ice when you first meet someone? How does physical touch make people feel more at ease? _____

_____

_____

_____

> *Prime Prayer:* Pray to remember to extend your hand to someone when you first meet, as if to say "I'm happy to know you."

Thursday

Jesus is our role model for hand handling! He used His hands over and over for three specific purposes, all of them producing comfort in the lives of those He touched. Read Matthew 9:27–30. Here Jesus used hands to _____. Read Matthew 17:5–8. This time He used them to _____. Last, Matthew 19:13–15. Jesus used His hands to _____ for others. List three ways you could use your hands the same ways Jesus used His. __

_____

_____

_____

Prime Prayer: Ask Jesus to help you reach out and lay your hands on your hurting friends to pray for them, asking Him to heal them, or hold them to help chase away their fears.

Friday

To cleanse your hands means more than just giving them a good washing with soap and water. James talks about cleansing hands in this different way. Read James 4:8. Here the phrase *cleanse your hands* means to keep from sinning. It means not to participate in anything evil, filthy, or ungodly. What are four ways a person could get his hands spiritually dirty? If you have "dirty" hands, use 1 John 1:9 to clean them up! _____

_____

_____

_____

Prime Prayer: Ask God to make you more aware of your hands so you can keep them spiritually clean by asking forgiveness for your sins.

■■■■■■■■■■■■■■■■■■■■■■■■■■■■■■■■■■■■■■■

THIS WEEK'S MEMORY VERSE: PICK IT! WRITE IT! REMEMBER IT!

_____

_____

_____

_____

_____

■■■■■■■■■■■■■■■■■■■■■■■■■■■■■■■■■■■■■■■

Beating the Blues

Anxiety in the heart of a man weighs it down, but a good word makes it glad.

Proverbs 12:25 NAS

Jim felt sad. School wasn't going like it used to. He had always been a pretty good student, but this last semester was tough for him. It wasn't just that his conceited psychology teacher, Mr. Larson, was making life cruel for him because he didn't see eye-to-eye with his worldly viewpoints. It was also chemistry class. Jim couldn't make up his mind which combustive chemical to report on, making his last-minute paper a flop. He was falling so far behind. Jim's heart was heavy. He felt so down about school. For the first time, he wondered whether he was going to crash and burn this semester, sending his hard-earned GPA on a downward spiral.

But, the problem wasn't just school. Jim's friendship with Mike was getting to him. No matter what he did, Mike made it seem like he was always wrong and Mike was always right! Jim had enough put-downs to last all year. After a while, Jim just wasn't himself. He moped around, spending most of his time closed in his bedroom with his headset on. He didn't care about Mike and his friends the way he used to. Staying home was fine with him. Frankly speaking, Jim was depressed.

Have you recently felt like Jim? Are you down in the dumps? Got the blues? Are you struggling with depression and discouragement? Are you not acting like yourself? Feel like pulling away from everyone or going out and getting blasted to escape? You may be depressed! Proverbs 12:25 tells us that anxiety, worry, and depression make our heart feel like someone tied it to a big boulder and threw it in the lake! Depression is a common emotion among teens, but it doesn't need to stick around. There are ways to chase it out of your life.

How can your heavy heart lighten up? Scripture tells us that a good word of encouragement will do the trick. No one needs another put-down, they need a word to put them up! Where can we go to get a good, uplifting word that will take the weight off a heavy heart? Check these out:

First, the Bible can be your best friend when it comes to good, positive words. And it's always right there for you! Open up and start reading.

Second, your pastor, priest, or youth director is also familiar with the Bible and can share some Scriptures with you that will lift you up. Pastors have a gentle, listening ear. If they didn't care, they wouldn't be in that profession!

Third, to many schoolteachers and counselors, teaching is more than just a job. They love teens. Test the waters.

Open up a little bit and see if they respond with encouraging words and trust.

Fourth, parents and close friends know your moods and are sensitive to your feelings. They may have just the perfect word to cheer you up. If you're hanging out with downbeat kids, better think about switching friends.

Fifth is YOU! What you say to yourself in the silence of your mind will affect how you feel. Thoughts like, *I'm so dumb! I'm a nothing!* or *Life stinks!* won't make you feel better. Try, *I may have messed up, but next time I'll do better* or *I'm a good person, I know myself better than they do, things will get better with God's help.* Your self-talk has about a 99.9 percent effect on how you feel about yourself, your circumstances, and others in your life. Control your thoughts. Don't let them control you! Encouraging words will start the crane cranking to lift that heavy boulder off your heart and drop it on the head of depression itself!

> Dear Lord, sometimes life gets me down. It seems as if everything goes wrong. I know You want me to be happy, so when I turn to You and others who care, send encouraging words my way. And help me to be an encouragement to others. Amen.

Prime Time This Week

Depression doesn't have the right to control your life or that of a friend or family member. Overcoming depression takes effort and action. You must *choose* to attack feelings of depression. Force them out! You may have a hard time getting started—you will have to do what you don't *feel* like doing *before* you feel like doing it. So here we go—lights, camera, ACTION!

Monday

First off, always go to the Lord with your feelings and problems. He cares more than anyone! What do Psalm 34:18, 19 and Psalm 27:5 promise to God's people who are down in the dumps? _____

_____

_____

_____

Prime Prayer: Ask God to remind you at the times when you feel depressed that He is with you and will lift you up.

Tuesday

Life not going your way? Are your expectations unrealistic? Be flexible! Read Proverbs 16:9 and Isaiah 55:8, 9. You might make plans, but who determines the final outcome? Be accepting of the Lord's plans. Only He can see the big picture. _____

_____

_____

_____

Prime Prayer: Ask God to help you to be open to His plans for your day, your week, and your life, knowing He can be trusted with your life.

Wednesday

Do you have anhedonia? Huh? *Anhedonia* is an incapacity to experience joy in your life. Most depressed people don't feel too joyful. Where can you get joy? Read Psalm 16:11. Right now you are in God's presence! Draw your joy from Him. _____

_____

_____

_____

Prime Prayer: Pray that you will make more time to spend in God's presence—praying to and praising Him—so you will know real joy.

Thursday

A surefire way to get over being down is to get up and out! Increase your activities. Do stuff! Don't be alone, seek out positive people and fun activities. Plus, working out does wonders. Exercise releases depression-fighting hormones. Fifteen minutes a day will start brightening your outlook. Make a list of some activities you would like to get involved in. Also make a workout schedule for the week. Try a different form of exercise each day so you don't get bored (basketball, jumping rope, skating, biking, jogging, weight lifting). _____

_____

_____

_____

Prime Prayer: Ask God to help you get up and work out when you feel blue. Thank Him for making your body able to fight depression.

Friday

Are you still sitting in life's low seat? Don't be too proud or too afraid to seek professional help. We all have times in our lives when a trained counselor is necessary. Don't give up! Talk it over with your parents.

Prime Prayer: Ask God to put someone in your life who will understand what you are going through and who will help you work it out.

■■■■■■■■■■■■■■■■■■■■■■■■■■■■■■■■■■■

THIS WEEK'S MEMORY VERSE: PICK IT! WRITE IT! REMEMBER IT!

_____

_____

_____

_____

_____

■■■■■■■■■■■■■■■■■■■■■■■■■■■■■■■■■■■

Follow the Yellow Brick Road

Where there is no vision, the people perish: but he
that keepeth the law, happy is he.

Proverbs 29:18 KJV

■ ■

Remember the Scarecrow in *The Wizard of Oz?* When
Dorothy first met him, he seemed rather confused. When
she asked him which way to the Land of Oz where the
great Wizard lived, he pointed in two different directions.

Do you ever feel like that straw-stuffed Scarecrow? De-
ciding which road to take in your life is a major decision.
Today's world offers so many opportunities and choices.
Picking a path can get complicated. Yet, God's Word tells
us that without a vision, or direction, people perish—or
more simply put, they dry up and blow away!

One good way to get started on a direction is to set
goals. With set goals, you will have a sense of purpose,
something to work toward. Choose goals that are realistic.
If your goals are nearly impossible to meet, you will be

setting yourself up for failure. Then what? Stress! Set clear, realistic goals you can work toward and do your best to meet.

What areas can you set goals in? Any area! Scholastics, finances, fitness, career direction, school and community involvement, or spiritual goals, just to name a few.

You can set weekly, monthly, or yearly goals—whatever suits you—whatever keeps you striving for that goal. Chris likes setting short goals. He says that short goals give him a greater chance of success. Plus every time he accomplishes a goal, it's a boost to his self-image.

Larry feels the same way. Short, obtainable goals make him feel better about himself. His increased confidence encourages him to set even greater goals.

Your goals don't have to be complicated. They can be simple, such as being nice to your brother or sister, showing up for class every day, finishing the book you started reading, or keeping your room clean. Well, to some teens these are complicated! Just don't think that your goals are irrelevant. If they matter to you, they are important and valid!

Also, set some long-term goals. Ask yourself what you want to be doing in one year, three years, five years, and ten years from now. Write your answers down and save them. You are not writing your future in cement, but you are giving yourself a direction.

Dear Jesus, I feel as if my life is going in ten different directions. I really want to know in which direction You want me to go. Open my eyes so I'll see Your leading. Amen.

Prime Time This Week

"Just follow the yellow brick road!" How nice for Glenda, the good witch, to direct Dorothy to her goal. Those little munchkins piped in, too! "Follow, follow, follow, follow, follow the yellow brick road!" Can't you just hear the tune in your head? Well, if only life were that simple. Jesus doesn't lay out the specifics of every person's life in the Bible, yet the Bible does give us some general instructions, some goals to strive for. This week find out what some of them are, then follow!

Monday

Here's one of Jesus' top priorities for your life. Read Mark 16:15–18 and Matthew 28:18–20. Preach, teach, baptize, make disciples, and pray. Why are these things so important to the Lord? How can you start putting them into practice today? Pick a friend and tell him or her about Jesus today! _____

_____

_____

Prime Prayer: Ask the Lord to help you realize that telling others about Him is not just the job of ministers or those fanatical Christians, but it's what He wants even *you* to do.

Tuesday

Your life is made up of activities and actions! Jesus has something specific to say about how He wants you to act toward others as you go through life. Read Luke 6:31–35. How can you put this into action? Are there some people you have been mistreating? Who? Write out a plan to start changing your actions. _____

_____

_____

> *Prime Prayer:* Ask the Lord to give you the maturity and strength to treat others lovingly, fairly, and kindly, just as you want to be treated.

Wednesday

SEX! Safe or not, God says, "NO." Premarital sex is not part of His plan for your life. Read 1 Thessalonians 4:3. But God's Word is not just full of "do not's!" For a great list of *do's* in life, get comfortable and read Jesus' Sermon on the Mount in Matthew 5, 6, and 7. List at least eight things this instructs you to *do*. _____

_____

_____

_____

Prime Prayer: Ask Jesus to help you concentrate on all of the *do's* in the Bible so the *do not's* won't seem at all tempting!

Thursday

Read Matthew 6:10. Jesus instructs His believers to pray for God's will to be done in their lives. That goes for you, too. Don't just wing it! Even Jesus got alone to pray for His Father's will to be done in His life, and He followed God's leading. Read about it in Luke 22:41–43. Why do you think God wants you to follow His will for you? _____

_____

_____

_____

Prime Prayer: Pray for God's will to be done in your life each day and that you will be able to accept His will and be obedient to it just as Jesus was.

Friday

What? Jesus wants you to pray? And He wants you to stay away from tempting situations? Read it yourself in Luke 22:46. How can prayer keep you from giving in to tempting situations? _____

_____

_____

_____

Prime Prayer: Thank God today that prayer gives you the strength to stay away from things that are not pleasing to God!

■■■■■■■■■■■■■■■■■■■■■■■■■■■■■■■■■■■■

THIS WEEK'S MEMORY VERSE: PICK IT! WRITE IT! REMEMBER IT!

_____

_____

_____

_____

_____

■■■■■■■■■■■■■■■■■■■■■■■■■■■■■■■■■■■■

Splinters for Jesus

Don't copy the behavior and customs of this world,
but be a new and different person with a fresh new-
ness in all you do and think. Then you will learn
from your own experience how his ways will really
satisfy you.

Romans 12:2 TLB

■■■■■■■■■■■■■■■■■■■■■■■■■■■■■■■■■■■

Have you ever stepped down on some rough old wood
or run your fingers up an aged boat paddle? How about a
dry stick or a small wooden match? What happens nine
times out of ten? You get a splinter! If you touch the object
in the same direction of the wood's grain, no big deal. No
splinter. It's when you go against the grain that a sharp
thin sliver of wood is forced straight into your flesh.
OUCH! Just the thought of it can send a chill up your
spine!

Many times in our Christian life we have to go against
the grain because it's what Jesus wants from us. If we drift
along with the crowd to be popular or to fit in, doing
things just because we think everyone else is (sometimes

167

they're not), we won't get any splinters, but we also won't feel very close to God or very much joy on the inside.

Romans 12:2 beckons us not to blend in with the crowd and do what they're doing when we know it's wrong. The world is supposed to see a visible difference between Christians and non-Christians. We, as Christians now have the ability and motivation to be new and changed people through the power of the Holy Spirit within us. When we go against the crowd, we may lose a few so-called friends, get called a "goody-goody," or spend some Saturday nights at home with Mom and Dad. Those are splinters! Yet, doing these things for our Lord will teach us how following His ways will bring us true happiness. When you get a splinter for Jesus, His abundant love, like a big pair of tweezers, will quickly come to remove the splinter and the pain and replace it with His gentle touch.

Jesus, splinters hurt, but I know that I'm not really happy or doing Your will when I mess up with my friends or in my thoughts toward others. Give me the courage to go against the grain for You. Amen.

Prime Time This Week

Standing out for Jesus has never been the way to win a popularity contest. Jesus, Himself, knew it wouldn't be. He knew His followers would be made fun of and criticized for their dedication to Him. It makes them stand out and be noticed because they are different. Christians are no longer the same. They've been changed on the inside. Jesus has made us new and fresh. Our behavior needs to reflect that change. Let's see how this week goes.

Monday

Accepting Jesus makes you a *new* person on the inside. Things are not the same, they're better. Read 2 Corinthians 5:17–20. What old things in your life need to pass away? What is an ambassador? How are you an ambassador for Jesus? _____

_____

_____

_____

Prime Prayer: Ask God for strength to get rid of old habits and ungodly actions so you can be a true representative of Him.

Tuesday

As you get closer to Jesus, you realize there are things He doesn't want you to do, so you stop. But, how will your friends react? Read 1 Peter 4:1–5. Who do they eventually have to answer to? Read 2 Corinthians 6:14 to see

why you and your old friends don't mix well any longer!
Write the reason here. _____

_____

_____

Prime Prayer: Ask God for courage as you step out of
your old circle of friends and into a new one!

Wednesday

Do your non-Christian peers ever try to intimidate you
because of your beliefs? Read 1 Peter 3:13–16. How can
you keep from being accused of being a fake? What happens when you suffer for Jesus? _____

_____

_____

Prime Prayer: Ask the Holy Spirit to keep you strong,
yet gentle when you have to explain yourself to others and to keep your conscience clear. Don't give in.
You'll be blessed.

Thursday

Can a person love the world and love the Lord at the
same time? Read 1 John 2:15–17. What are the three things

from the world, not from God? If we indulge in these things, we make ourselves a friend to the world. Check out James 4:4. How does friendship with the things of the world affect your relationship with God? _____

_____

_____

_____

Prime Prayer: Ask God to teach you how to keep Him as your first love and to help you desire only Him.

Friday

Peer pressure gets tough. Jesus knows! He was pressured by Satan, but He never gave in. Finally what did the devil do? Read Matthew 4:1–11. _____

_____

_____

_____

Prime Prayer: Pray for persistence in resisting Satan so he'll finally give up. Start praising God and Satan will run!

■■■■■■■■■■■■■■■■■■■■■■■■■■■■■■■■■■■■

THIS WEEK'S MEMORY VERSE: PICK IT! WRITE IT! REMEMBER IT!

_____

_____

_____

_____

_____

■■■■■■■■■■■■■■■■■■■■■■■■■■■■■■■■■■■■

Holy Hank

Try to stay out of quarrels and seek to live a clean and holy life. . . .

Hebrews 12:14 TLB

■■■■■■■■■■■■■■■■■■■■■■■■■■■■■■■■■■■■■■■

Hank had just turned down another invitation to a hot party next weekend. Sometimes it just killed him on the inside. It was hard to say no because he liked being with his classmates. But Hank had made a commitment to Christ to be an example of Him. He knew it was best to steer clear of situations that could be trouble. Saying no, however, wasn't the only tough thing for Hank. It was the way his friends had started to tease him. They couldn't quite understand Hank's new life-style. He was good-looking, well-liked, a class officer, and played a mean keyboard. He also cared for others, always helping out wherever he could.

But Hank kept himself separated when he knew God wanted him to. For this the kids at school had nicknamed him Holy Hank. Normally when teens take a stand for Christ, they don't fit in with their old friends. They're different. They don't hang out, go to the wild parties, do drugs, and so on. As in Hank's situation, other students start talking behind their backs saying things like, "So, Hank thinks he's too good for us now" or "He's on some religious kick, he'll get over it."

In reality, teens like Hank are only doing what God has asked. Hank *is* being holy. Holy simply means set apart from the rest of the world. They should see a visible difference in what *Christians* do and say.

Holiness also means to be morally pure. With God's help, we are to be obedient to God's Word, making a constant effort to stay away from sin. Sound impossible in today's immoral and polluted world? That's why Hebrews 12:14 says to seek or pursue holiness. The word *pursue* means to keep going, keep striving. It is a process. If at first you don't succeed, try, try, again! That's exactly what Hank was doing. And if others want to tease him and call him Holy Hank, more power to him!

Dear Lord, help me to choose in my heart to live a life that will be separated for You. Please keep me strong when my friends don't understand my beliefs. I love You. Amen.

Prime Time This Week

Several places in the Bible, God tells Christians to be holy because He is holy. To state it simply, God is asking us to be like Him. That's a natural desire of a father. God *is* our heavenly Father. If we grow up like Him, He'll be able to look at us proudly and say, "Yep, that's my boy." In response to that kind of love, you and I desire to please Him, obey His Word, and be holy. This week let's look at the idea of holiness and what it means in your teen years.

Monday

To be holy is to be like the character of God. To be the kind of person God is, we are to be opposite or separate from evil and worldliness. Read 2 Corinthians 6:14–18 and 1 Peter 2:9. How do these verses describe God's people? How are we different from others? _____

_____

_____

_____

Prime Prayer: Ask God to make you realize you are His, no longer in darkness, but in His light, made for the purpose of bringing His light to others.

Tuesday

The Apostle Paul tells us what holiness is *not* in order to help us better understand what it is. Read 1 Thessalonians 4:3–7 (*sanctification* means holiness). Now see

Colossians 3:5–10. List the characteristics given that are not holy. _____

_____

_____

_____

> *Prime Prayer:* Ask God to help you remain pure in
> your thoughts and actions and ask Him to forgive
> you for your wrongs in this area, if needed.

Wednesday

As you are pursuing holiness, you'll find it is humanly impossible to be 100 percent sin-free! That's one reason why Jesus died for our sins—so we could have forgiveness and grace! Read Paul's struggle with being holy in Romans 7:15–8:2. And when you do mess up, check out 1 John 1:9. Do you ever feel like Paul? Explain your battle with holiness. _____

_____

_____

_____

> *Prime Prayer:* Thank God right now for providing for-
> giveness through His Son, Jesus, so you can keep
> striving to be holy.

Thursday

Why does God want us to be holy? So we'll be like Him. Yet there are more reasons! The holier or cleaner we are to God, the more useful we will be to His service. Read 2 Timothy 2:21. As you get closer to God, how do you think He might use you for His purposes? Now keep reading through verse 23. What four things does God want you to go after? _____

_____

_____

_____

Prime Prayer: Ask God to help you try to be a vessel for honor and service to Him.

Friday

Joy, joy, joy! God's reason for wanting us to be holy isn't just so we'll please Him and so the world will know we are different. It's also for us! Holiness, which is also obedience to God's Word, will fill you with joy and God's love. Read John 15:10, 11. List an example of when you felt good because you knew you did the right thing. _____

_____

_____

_____

Prime Prayer: Pray that your heart will be filled with joy because you are living in God's love and doing what pleases Him.

■■■■■■■■■■■■■■■■■■■■■■■■■■■■■■■■■■■■

THIS WEEK'S MEMORY VERSE: PICK IT! WRITE IT! REMEMBER IT!

_____

_____

_____

_____

_____

■■■■■■■■■■■■■■■■■■■■■■■■■■■■■■■■■■■■

Has your study time challenged you and made you think about your life and important issues in a new way? Do you have some tough questions that need answers? Terrific! Asking questions shows you care. If you need help getting those questions answered, please write. We will do our best to help you out. We look forward to hearing from you!

Reverend Bill and Andrea Stephens
P.O. Box 3080
Covington, LA 70434